BODYBUILDING ANATOMY

Nick Evans

Illustrated by
William P. Hamilton

Human Kinetics

Library of Congress Cataloging-in-Publication Data

Evans, Nick, 1964-
  Bodybuilding anatomy / Nick Evans.
     p. cm.
  Includes index.
  ISBN-13: 978-0-7360-5926-8 (soft cover)
  ISBN-10: 0-7360-5926-1 (soft cover)
  1. Bodybuilding. 2. Muscles--Anatomy. 3. Muscle strength. I. Title.

  GV546.5.E82 2007
  613.7'13--dc22

                                        2006013855

ISBN-10: 0-7360-5926-1
ISBN-13: 978-0-7360-5926-8

Acquisitions Editor: Martin Barnard; **Developmental Editor:** Leigh Keylock; **Assistant Editor:** Christine Horger; **Copyeditor:** Jan Feeney; **Proofreader:** Erin Cler; **Graphic Designer:** Fred Starbird; **Graphic Artist:** Francine Hamerski; **Cover Designer:** Keith Blomberg; **Art Manager:** Kelly Hendren; **Illustrator (cover and interior):** © 2007 William P. Hamilton; **Printer:** United Graphics

Human Kinetics books are available at special discounts for bulk purchase. Special editions or book excerpts can also be created to specification. For details, contact the Special Sales Manager at Human Kinetics.

Printed in the United States of America   10   9   8   7   6

The paper in this book is certified under a sustainable forestry program.

Human Kinetics
Web site: www.HumanKinetics.com

United States: Human Kinetics
P.O. Box 5076
Champaign, IL 61825-5076
800-747-4457
e-mail: humank@hkusa.com

Canada: Human Kinetics
475 Devonshire Road, Unit 100
Windsor, ON N8Y 2L5
800-465-7301 (in Canada only)
e-mail: info@hkcanada.com

Europe: Human Kinetics
107 Bradford Road
Stanningley
Leeds LS28 6AT, United Kingdom
+44 (0)113 255 5665
e-mail: hk@hkeurope.com

Australia: Human Kinetics
57A Price Avenue
Lower Mitcham, South Australia 5062
08 8372 0999
e-mail: info@hkaustralia.com

New Zealand: Human Kinetics
P.O. Box 80
Torrens Park, South Australia 5062
0800 222 062
e-mail: info@hknewzealand.com

CONTENTS

PREFACE

Walk into any gym these days and it's like Disneyland for bodybuilders. You'll discover endless rows of exercise machines and free weights for every muscle in your body. Your challenge is to navigate through the maze of machines and weights, select the exercises you need, and pump your way across the gym to the finish line. Upside: The winner walks away with a custom-built body. Downside: No instructions, no clues, no map, and no rules. But with no guidance, surely you're doomed to circulate around the gym, stuck in a holding pattern. Then one lucky day, in a moment of clarity, you realize a piece of the puzzle is missing.

Today is your lucky day! You've found the missing piece: *Bodybuilding Anatomy,* a book of instructions for every exercise in the gym. Go ahead and check it out for yourself. Flip open the book and pick a page—any page you want. Now, let's see what you get. Each exercise is illustrated in amazing detail with a picture that's worth a thousand words, revealing the anatomy under your skin: the main muscles at work and those muscles that assist during the exercise. Alongside the illustration are step-by-step instructions on how to perfect your exercise technique. What's more, you'll find a list of advanced technical tricks to modify the exercise for maximum effect. You'll learn how to adjust your grip, where to position your feet, and how to position your body. You'll discover how to manipulate exercise trajectory and range of motion in order to emphasize different sections of the targeted muscle. Whatever choice you face at the gym—barbells or dumbbells, free weights or machines, wide grip or narrow grip, incline or decline, sitting or standing—you'll get all the help you need. No weight plate is left unturned.

You can review any exercise in this book in under five minutes. During that short time, you'll discover and learn everything you need to know to make your workouts more precise. This book will shift your training up a gear, and then some.

It's no secret what you want from your workouts: a custom-built body. But in order to change the way you look, you must modify your anatomy. You should skillfully use weights to sculpt your body, not just to indiscriminately pack on pounds of flesh. The real secret is that to change anatomy, you must first *know* anatomy!

Bodybuilding Anatomy is the ultimate reference, loaded with detailed technical discussions and illustrated with anatomical precision. The book is systematically organized into muscle groups, so finding the exercises you need in order to build any muscle is easy. What's more, each body part is subdivided even further into target zones, allowing you to select the specific exercises you need to target hard-to-hit spots in your physique.

Chapter 1 serves up shoulders—boulderlike shoulders that form the cornerstones of a great physique. You'll discover the anatomy and develop a strategy to detonate your deltoids. Simply packing the plates on a shoulder press is not enough. When you know shoulder anatomy, you'll realize that each of the three sections of the deltoid muscle demands a different exercise. Also, this chapter reveals the secrets to a strong, injury-resistant rotator cuff.

In chapter 2, you will discover how to hammer and chisel the chest. You will analyze the anatomy and evaluate the exercises that you need to plump up your pectorals. You'll work all the angles, change your grip, and manipulate the movements to carve up your chest. With these technically precise exercises in your chest workout, you'll build a breastplate of armor that would make any gladiator proud!

Chapter 3 takes you around the back. Three slabs of muscle cover your back. If you train only the lats, your back workout is incomplete. To add thickness across your upper back, you need to target the trapezius. To create a foundation of strength in your lower back, you must work the erector spinae muscles. And when it comes to latissimus dorsi, you'll be shown how to perfect your pulldown and revamp your row to create that athletic V-shape taper.

In chapter 4, get ready to arm yourself with a pair of big guns. The triceps make up two-thirds of the muscle mass in your upper arm. You'll get all the growth-forging techniques to hammer more size into your triceps and beef up your biceps. You'll also get a grip on the 10 ropelike muscles in your forearms that are on display whenever you wear a short-sleeved shirt.

Chapter 5 is all about legs. Whatever your pleasure—a quadriceps teardrop, an outer-thigh sweep, thicker hamstrings, bigger calves, or a tighter butt—this chapter teaches you how to adapt any leg exercise to meet your own needs.

Chapter 6 is devoted to the development of phenomenal abdominals. You'll get the anatomic treasure map to the three zones of your midsection: the upper abs, the lower abs, and the obliques. Each muscle zone has a different set of exercise requirements. This chapter delivers all the crunches, raises, twists, and turns you need in order to sculpt a sizzling six-pack.

You'd better believe it: Knowledge of anatomy is the key for any serious bodybuilder. Muscular proportion and symmetry are created by intelligent exercise choices, not by chance. It doesn't matter how much workout experience you have; this book will help you customize your body with the skill of a master mechanic. The next time you set foot in the gym, you'll have a new set of rules to lift by. And by taking the guesswork out of bodybuilding, your efforts at the gym will be more productive and efficient—maximum results in minimum time!

If you are one of the millions of people who work out, this is a book you can't afford to be without. Like having an X ray of each exercise, *Bodybuilding Anatomy* provides an inside view of your muscles in action. This ultimate bodybuilding reference contains detailed, full-color anatomical drawings of exercises that target every major muscle group. Armed with advanced tricks and modifications to isolate specific muscles, you will learn how to tweak your technique and fine-tune your physique. This book is a must for everyone's gym bag!

The shoulder is a "ball-and-socket" joint between the humerus bone of the upper arm and the scapula bone (shoulder blade). Six main movements occur at the shoulder: flexion, extension, abduction, adduction, internal rotation, and external rotation. During shoulder flexion, the upper arm is elevated forward toward the face. During shoulder extension, the arm moves backward behind the plane of the body. During abduction, the arm moves up and out to the side of the body. During adduction, the arm is pulled in toward the side of the body. Horizontal abduction and adduction occur when the arm moves in a horizontal plane at shoulder level, such as during chest flys or rear deltoid flys.

The deltoid muscle of the shoulder consists of three separate sections, or heads, each capable of moving the arm in different directions. From a broad tendon attachment above the shoulder joint, the deltoid's three heads merge into a single tendon that attaches to the humerus bone of the upper arm. The anterior deltoid (in front) attaches to the clavicle and raises the arm forward (shoulder flexion). The lateral deltoid (at the side) attaches to the acromion and lifts the arm outward to the side (abduction). The posterior deltoid (behind) attaches to the scapula and moves the arm backward (shoulder extension).

The rotator cuff is a group of four muscles that form a protective sleeve around the shoulder joint. Despite being a barely visible muscle group, the rotator cuff is essential for shoulder stability and strength. All four muscles originate from the scapula (shoulder blade) and pass across the shoulder joint to attach onto the humerus bone of the upper arm. The supraspinatus lies above the joint and raises (abducts) the arm up and outward—as when hailing a taxi. Infraspinatus and teres minor are located behind and act to rotate the arm out—as when hitchhiking. Subscapularis is situated in front and rotates the arm inward—as when folding your arms across the chest.

Anatomy of the Deltoid, Front View

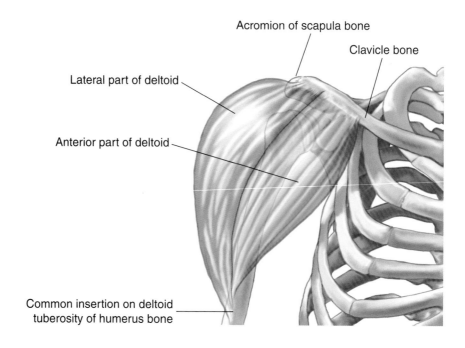

Acromion of scapula bone

Clavicle bone

Lateral part of deltoid

Anterior part of deltoid

Common insertion on deltoid tuberosity of humerus bone

Anatomy of the Deltoid, Rear View

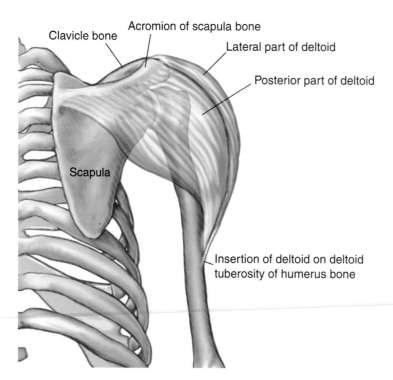

Acromion of scapula bone

Clavicle bone

Lateral part of deltoid

Posterior part of deltoid

Scapula

Insertion of deltoid on deltoid tuberosity of humerus bone

Anatomy of the Rotator Cuff, Front View

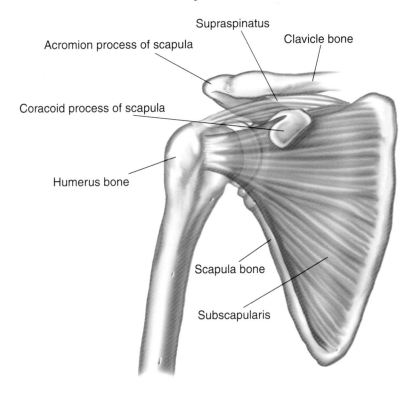

Suprasinatus

Acromion process of scapula

Clavicle bone

Coracoid process of scapula

Humerus bone

Scapula bone

Subscapularis

Anatomy of the Rotator Cuff, Rear View

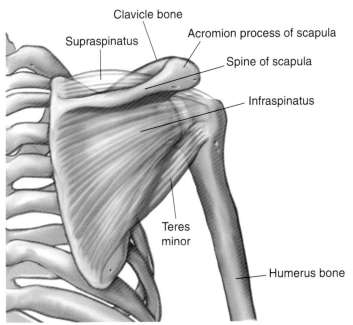

Clavicle bone

Supraspinatus

Acromion process of scapula

Spine of scapula

Infraspinatus

Teres minor

Humerus bone

Barbell Shoulder Press

FINISH

Anterior deltoid

Triceps

START

Upper pectoralis

Execution

1. Seated on a bench, take a shoulder-width grip on the bar with your palms facing forward.
2. Lower the weight slowly (in front) until it touches your upper chest.
3. Push vertically upward until your elbows lock out.

Muscles Involved

Primary: Anterior deltoid.

Secondary: Lateral deltoid, triceps, trapezius, and upper pectoralis.

Anatomic Focus

Hand spacing: A shoulder-width grip is preferred to target the anterior deltoid. Wider grips on the bar minimize triceps contribution, but as the grip gets wider the risk of shoulder injury increases.

Range of motion: A shorter rep terminating the press just before lockout keeps tension on the deltoid.

Positioning: Performing the exercise while seated upright is a stricter version than standing and prevents cheating the weight upward using momentum generated by the legs.

VARIATIONS

Machine Shoulder Press

Machines provide better stability and safety and offer a choice of handgrips. A neutral grip (palms facing together) targets the anterior deltoid better than a pronated grip (palms forward).

Neutral grip

Pronated grip

Additional variation:

Behind-the-neck press: This version places the shoulder in more external rotation, and the risk of shoulder injury is greater when the weight is lifted behind the neck.

Dumbbell Shoulder Press

FINISH

Lateral deltoid

Anterior deltoid

Triceps

START

Posterior deltoid

Trapezius

Execution

1. Seated on a bench, begin with the dumbbells at shoulder level, palms facing forward.
2. Press the dumbbells vertically upward until your elbows lock out.
3. Lower the dumbbells back down until they touch your shoulders.

Muscles Involved

Primary: Anterior deltoid.

Secondary: Lateral deltoid, triceps, trapezius, upper pectoralis.

Anatomic Focus

Grip: Changing the orientation of the dumbbells affects hand position (grip). Pressing the dumbbells upward with palms facing forward (pronated grip) works both the anterior and the lateral heads of the deltoid. Pressing the

dumbbells with palms facing together (neutral grip) makes the anterior deltoid work harder, minimizing lateral head involvement. Holding the dumbbells with palms facing backward (supinated grip) maximizes anterior deltoid effort.

Positioning: Performing the exercise while seated upright is a stricter version than standing and prevents cheating the dumbbells upward using momentum.

VARIATIONS

Variable-Grip Dumbbell Press

This version uses three different hand positions during the repetition. Begin the exercise by holding the dumbbells with your palms facing back (supination). During the press, rotate the dumbbells so your palms face together (neutral grip) at the midpoint, finishing the upward press with your palms facing forward (pronated grip) at lockout.

Additional variation:

Alternating one-arm dumbbell press: Perform the exercise by pressing one dumbbell at a time, alternating right arm then left arm.

Dumbbell Front Raise

Lateral deltoid

Upper pectoralis

Anterior deltoid

FINISH

START

Execution

1. Sitting upright on the edge of an exercise bench, hold a pair of dumbbells at arms' length by your sides, thumbs pointing forward.
2. Lift one dumbbell out in front up toward shoulder level, keeping your elbow stiff.
3. Lower the weight back down to the start position, and repeat with the other dumbbell.

Muscles Involved

Primary: Anterior deltoid.

Secondary: Upper pectoralis, trapezius.

Anatomic Focus

Grip: A neutral grip (palm inward, thumb pointing forward) emphasizes the anterior deltoid. A pronated grip (palm down) allows the lateral deltoid to assist.

VARIATION

Variable-Grip Dumbbell Front Raise

Begin with a neutral grip (thumb forward), then rotate the dumbbell through 90 degrees during the lift so that your grip is pronated (palm down) at the top.

Barbell Front Raise

Upper pectoralis

Anterior deltoid

Lateral deltoid

Posterior deltoid

Trapezius

FINISH

START

Execution

1. Using an overhand shoulder-width grip, hold a barbell at arms' length in front of your thighs.
2. Raise the barbell forward and upward to eye level, keeping your elbows stiff.
3. Lower the barbell back down to your thighs.

Muscles Involved

Primary: Anterior deltoid.

Secondary: Lateral deltoid, trapezius, upper pectoralis.

Anatomic Focus

Hand spacing: Narrow hand spacing emphasizes the anterior deltoid, whereas a wider grip requires lateral deltoid assistance.

VARIATION

Single Dumbbell Front Raise

Grab a dumbbell with both hands, interlocking your fingers around the handle. The neutral grip (thumbs pointing forward) and narrow hand spacing target the anterior deltoid, minimizing involvement of the lateral deltoid.

Cable Front Raise

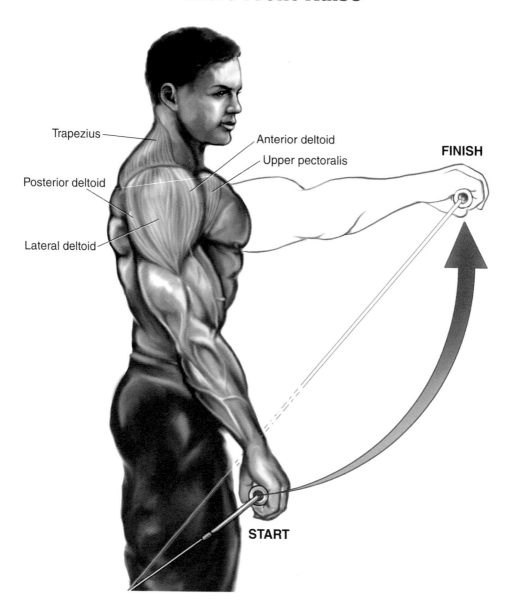

Trapezius

Posterior deltoid

Lateral deltoid

Anterior deltoid

Upper pectoralis

FINISH

START

Execution

1. With one hand, grab the D-handle attached to a low pulley, using a pronated grip (palm down).
2. Facing away from the weight stack, raise the handle in an upward arc to shoulder level, keeping the elbow stiff.
3. Lower the handle back down to waist level.

Muscles Involved

Primary: Anterior deltoid.

Secondary: Lateral deltoid, trapezius, upper pectoralis.

Anatomic Focus

Grip: The pronated overhand grip works the anterior and lateral heads of the deltoid.

VARIATIONS

Short Bar Attachment

Facing away from the machine with the cable running between your legs, grab the bar with both hands, using a shoulder-width overhand grip.

Additional variation:

Rope attachment: Facing away from the machine with the cable running between your legs, grab the rope ends with both hands, thumbs pointing upward.

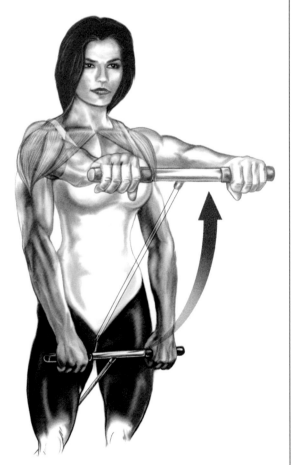

Dumbbell Lateral Raise

Anterior deltoid

Lateral deltoid

Posterior deltoid

FINISH

START

Execution

1. While standing upright, hold dumbbells at arms' length.
2. Raise arms out to the side in an arc until dumbbells reach shoulder level.
3. Lower dumbbells back down to hips.

Muscles Involved

Primary: Lateral deltoid.

Secondary: Anterior deltoid, posterior deltoid, trapezius, supraspinatus.

Anatomic Focus

Range of motion: The lateral deltoid performs most of the work as the dumbbells are raised up to shoulder level. The trapezius takes over if the dumbbells are raised higher, so terminating the upward phase at shoulder level keeps tension on the deltoid.

Grip: Effort from the lateral deltoid is maximized when the dumbbells are held parallel to the floor. Tilting the dumbbells with thumbs up externally rotates the shoulder and makes the anterior deltoid contribute to the motion, whereas tilting the dumbbells with thumbs down internally rotates the shoulder, allowing the posterior deltoid to assist.

Grip with external or internal rotation

Trajectory: Lifting the dumbbells directly out to the side hits the lateral deltoid. Raising the dumbbells from in front of the hips with a forward arc makes the anterior deltoid assist. If the arc of motion occurs behind the plane of the body, then the posterior deltoid contributes to the lift.

In front of the hips or behind the body

Resistance: Because of the effect of gravity on the dumbbells, resistance is lower at the beginning of the movement and gradually increases to a maximum as the dumbbells are raised to shoulder level.

VARIATIONS

Seated dumbbell lateral raise: Performing the dumbbell lateral raise seated on a flat exercise bench is a stricter version of the standing dumbbell lateral raise, minimizing the use of momentum to swing the dumbbells upward.

One-arm dumbbell lateral raise: You can perform this exercise using one arm at a time, stabilizing your torso with your free hand.

Cable Lateral Raise

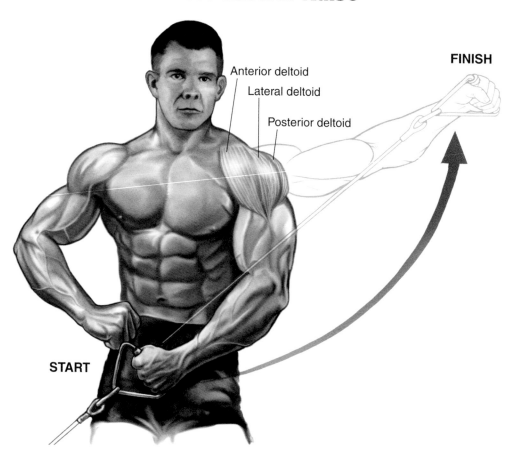

FINISH

Anterior deltoid

Lateral deltoid

Posterior deltoid

START

Execution

1. With one hand, grasp the D-handle attached to a low pulley.
2. Raise hand outward in a wide arc up to shoulder level, keeping the elbow stiff.
3. Lower the handle back down to waist level.

Muscles Involved

Primary: Lateral deltoid.

Secondary: Anterior deltoid, posterior deltoid, trapezius, supraspinatus.

Anatomic Focus

Range of motion: Terminating the upward phase at shoulder height keeps tension on the lateral deltoid. If the handle is raised higher, the trapezius takes over the work. The supraspinatus assists the lateral deltoid during the first 30 degrees of the movement. Starting the repetition with your hand in front of the opposite thigh can increase the range of motion by extending the early phase of the movement.

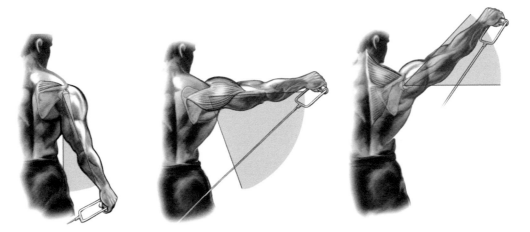

A higher finish recruits the trapezius.

Trajectory: The lateral deltoid is targeted best when the hand is raised directly out to the side. Performing the raise in front of the plane of your body activates the anterior deltoid, whereas raising your hand from the rear activates the posterior deltoid.

Resistance: Unlike dumbbell lateral raises, where the resistance varies during the lift, the cable pulley provides uniform resistance throughout the motion.

Machine Lateral Raise

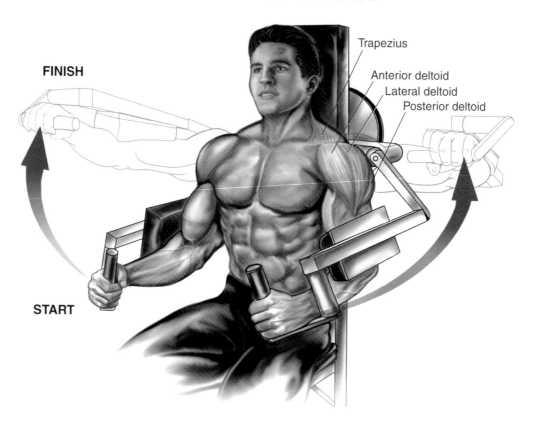

FINISH

Trapezius

Anterior deltoid
Lateral deltoid
Posterior deltoid

START

Execution

1. Sit on the machine with your elbows against the pads, and grasp the handles.
2. Raise your elbows to shoulder level, upper arms parallel to the floor.
3. Lower elbows back down to your sides.

Muscles Involved

Primary: Lateral deltoid.

Secondary: Anterior deltoid, posterior deltoid, trapezius, supraspinatus.

Anatomic Focus

Range of motion: Machine raises provide a uniform resistance throughout the movement. The supraspinatus assists at the start, and the trapezius assists if the elbows are raised above shoulder level.

Grip: A pronated grip (palms down) internally rotates the shoulder and targets the lateral deltoid. A neutral grip (palms facing in) or supinated grip (palms up) externally rotates the shoulder and increases the contribution of the anterior deltoid. Changes in shoulder rotation are made easier by gripping the elbow pads and *not* holding onto the machine's handles.

Trajectory: Altering the trajectory of the lift changes the relative focus on the deltoid. Raising your elbows directly out to the sides hits the lateral deltoid. Performing the raise with your elbows positioned forward on the pads makes the anterior deltoid assist.

VARIATION

One-Arm Machine Lateral Raise

You can perform this exercise using one arm at a time to improve focus and isolation. Some machines are designed so that you face inward, stabilizing your torso against a chest pad.

Barbell Upright Row

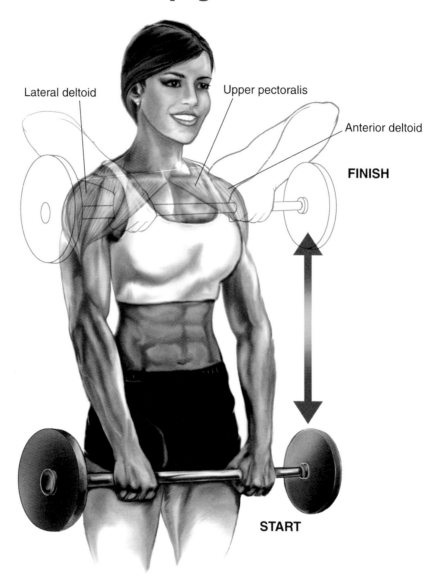

Lateral deltoid

Upper pectoralis

Anterior deltoid

FINISH

START

Execution

1. Hold a barbell at arms' length using an overhand shoulder-width grip.
2. Pull the bar vertically upward, raising the elbows to shoulder height.
3. Lower the bar slowly down to the arms' extended position.

Muscles Involved

Primary: Lateral deltoid, trapezius.

Secondary: Anterior deltoid, supraspinatus, infraspinatus, teres minor.

Anatomic Focus

Hand spacing: Taking a wider grip on the bar helps target the deltoid, whereas a narrower grip emphasizes the trapezius.

Wide grip   **Narrow grip**

Trajectory: Lifting the barbell close to the body targets the lateral deltoid, whereas raising the bar through a forward arc away from the body requires assistance from the anterior deltoid.

Range of motion: If the elbows are raised above shoulder level, the trapezius takes over the work.

VARIATIONS

Cable upright row: Using a straight bar attached to the low pulley of a cable machine provides steady resistance throughout the movement.

Machine upright row: Using a Smith machine provides a single plane of vertical motion that may help focus your effort.

Bent-Over Dumbbell Raise

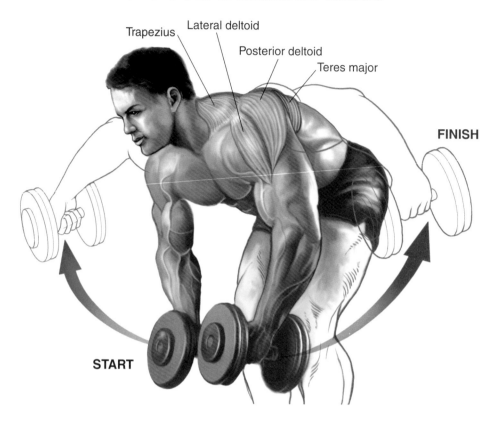

Trapezius
Lateral deltoid
Posterior deltoid
Teres major
FINISH
START

Execution

1. Holding two dumbbells at arms' length, bend forward at the waist, keeping your back straight and head up.
2. With palms facing together, raise dumbbells upward to ear level, keeping elbows slightly bent.
3. Lower dumbbells back down to start position.

Muscles Involved

Primary: Posterior deltoid.

Secondary: Lateral deltoid, trapezius, rhomboids, infraspinatus, teres minor, teres major.

Anatomic Focus

Grip: The way you hold the dumbbells influences the degree of rotation at the shoulder joint. Holding the dumbbells using a neutral grip (with thumbs pointing forward) allows the lateral deltoid to work in the exercise. A pronated grip on the dumbbells (with thumbs pointing inward) targets the posterior deltoid because the shoulder is rotated internally and the action of the lateral deltoid is reduced.

Resistance: Because of the effect of gravity on the dumbbells, the resistance is lower at the beginning of the movement and gradually increases to a maximum as the dumbbells are raised.

Trajectory: Altering the trajectory of the lift changes the relative focus on the deltoid. With your torso flat and parallel to the floor, emphasis is placed on the posterior deltoid. If your torso is inclined with your chest upright, the lateral deltoid contributes to the movement.

VARIATIONS

Head-Supported Dumbbell Raise

You can do this exercise with your forehead supported on the uppermost end of an incline exercise bench. Stand behind and in line with the bench, bend forward at the waist until your head touches the top of the backrest (which should be set at an appropriate height for your torso to be almost parallel to the floor). Supporting your head restricts movement in the spine and prevents swinging the dumbbells upward with momentum.

Head-supported dumbbell raise

Seated Bent-Over Dumbbell Raise

Sit on the end of an exercise bench while bent forward at the waist with your chest resting on the thighs. Note the pronated grip on the dumbbells (thumbs pointing inward), which improves isolation of the rear deltoid.

Seated bent-over dumbbell raise

Bent-Over Cable Raise

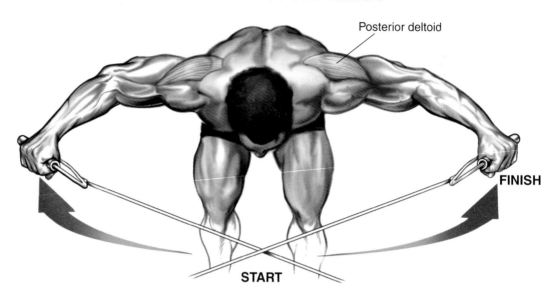

Execution

1. Grab the handles attached to two low pulleys (left-side handle in right hand, right-side handle in left hand), stand in the middle, then bend forward at the waist with back straight and parallel to the floor.

2. Raise your hands upward in an arc to shoulder level, such that the cables cross over.

3. Lower the handles back down to the start position, your right hand directly in front of the left ankle and your left hand in front of the right ankle.

Muscles Involved

Primary: Posterior deltoid.

Secondary: Lateral deltoid, trapezius, rhomboids, infraspinatus, teres minor, teres major.

Anatomic Focus

Trajectory: To target the posterior deltoid, your arms should move directly out to the sides. If your hands are raised in a forward arc in front of your head, the trapezius and lateral deltoid contribute to the exercise.

Body position: Isolation of the posterior deltoid is better with your torso parallel to the floor, not inclined with your chest and head uppermost.

Range of motion: The range of motion at the start is increased if the hands are allowed to cross over (uncrossing the cables) as the handles are lowered. The added distance and further stretch make the posterior deltoid work harder.

Resistance: Unlike dumbbell raises, where the resistance varies during the lift, the cable pulley affords a uniform resistance throughout the motion.

Grip: The cable handle does not allow you to make changes in hand position or grip.

VARIATION

One-Arm Bent-Over Cable Raise

You can do this exercise using one arm at a time, allowing you to alter the range of motion by adjusting the start or finish positions. This unilateral version makes it possible to raise your hand higher and get a longer stretch at the bottom, thereby generating more work for the posterior deltoid. Stabilize your torso by resting your free hand on the thigh.

Reverse Cable Crossover

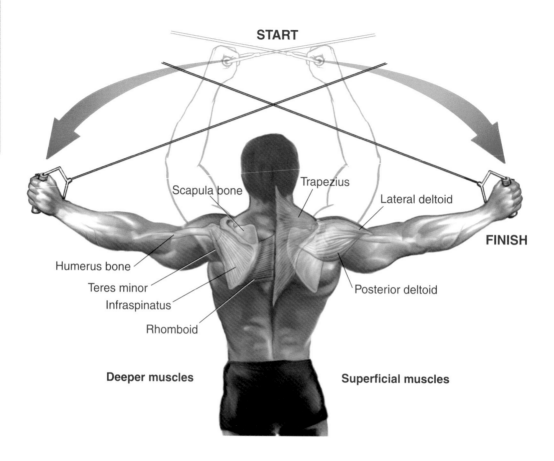

START

Scapula bone

Trapezius

Lateral deltoid

FINISH

Humerus bone

Teres minor

Infraspinatus

Rhomboid

Posterior deltoid

Deeper muscles

Superficial muscles

Execution

1. Using a thumbs-up grip, grab the handles attached to two high pulleys (left-side handle in right hand, right-side handle in left hand), stand upright and centrally with pulleys in front of you. (Note: during cable crossovers for chest, the pulleys are behind you.)

2. Pull your hands backward (and slightly down) in an arc, arms nearly parallel to the floor until your hands are in line with your shoulders (forming a T).

3. Return the handles back to the start position where your right hand is directly in front of the left shoulder and your left hand in front of the right shoulder.

Muscles Involved

Primary: Posterior deltoid.

Secondary: Lateral deltoid, trapezius, rhomboids, infraspinatus, teres minor, teres major.

Anatomic Focus

Trajectory: To target the posterior deltoid, your arms should move directly back (and downward slightly) almost parallel to the floor. If the hands are raised through a higher arc to a point above shoulder level, the trapezius and lateral deltoid make a bigger contribution to the movement.

Body position: The posterior deltoid is best targeted with your torso upright, not leaning too far forward or back.

Range: Crossing your hands over one another (uncrossing the cables) at the start position increases the range of motion and muscle stretch, thereby making the posterior deltoid work harder.

VARIATION

Supported reverse cable crossover: You can do this exercise (seated or standing) either with the chest supported on the backrest of an incline exercise bench or with the chest against the pad of a preacher bench. The bench is positioned centrally between two cable pulleys. Whether you sit on the bench or stand over it is optional, but you must be positioned high enough to allow the arms to perform the exercise without obstruction, with the pulleys level or just higher than your head. This variation is easier on your lower back, so you can focus on working the deltoid.

Machine Rear Deltoid Fly

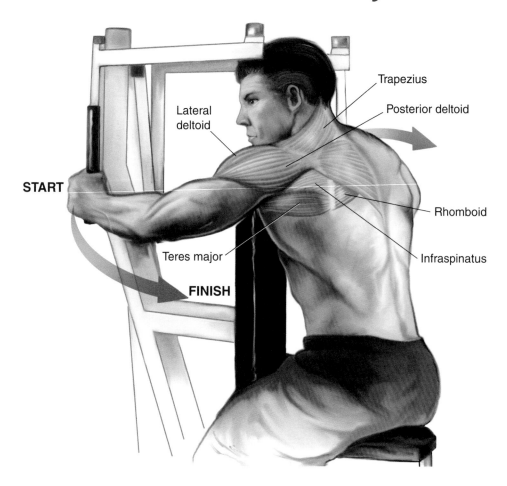

Execution

1. Sit facing the rear deltoid machine with your chest against the backrest, and grasp the handles directly in front with arms outstretched at shoulder level.
2. Pull the handles back in an arc as far as possible, keeping your elbows high and arms parallel to the floor.
3. Return the handles to the start position directly in front.

Muscles Involved

Primary: Posterior deltoid.

Secondary: Trapezius, rhomboids, lateral deltoid, infraspinatus, teres minor, teres major.

Anatomic Focus

Resistance: Like cable exercises, the rear deltoid fly machine provides a uniform resistance throughout the range of motion. This machine also offers several technical adjustments to grip, trajectory, and range of motion to help isolate the posterior deltoid.

Grip: Most modern rear deltoid fly machines provide a choice of handles: one pair horizontal and the other pair vertical. How you hold the handles affects the degree of rotation at the shoulder joint. Using the horizontal handles with a pronated grip (palms down) is the best method of isolating the posterior deltoid because the shoulder is internally rotated. A neutral grip (thumbs up) using the vertical handles allows the lateral deltoid to participate because the shoulder is externally rotated.

Pronated grip

Trajectory: Altering the trajectory of the lift changes the relative focus on the muscles. The posterior deltoid is worked best when the handles are grasped at or just below shoulder level, with your arms roughly parallel to the floor. If the handles are grasped above shoulder level, with the seat too low, then the trapezius performs a greater portion of the work during the exercise.

Range: You can increase the range of motion by performing the exercise with one arm at a time (see Variation section).

VARIATION

One-arm variation: Performing this exercise with one arm at a time reduces the relative contribution from the trapezius and the scapular retractor muscles, which thereby aids posterior deltoid isolation. You can also modify the range of motion during the one-arm version by changing your seating position on the machine. Sitting side-on with your inner shoulder against the backrest and performing the exercise using the outermost arm enable you to begin the exercise from a more distant start point beyond the opposite shoulder. This adjustment provides a greater stretch of the deltoid and increases the effective range of motion by as much as one third.

External Rotation

Supraspinatus
Spine of scapula bone
Infraspinatus
Teres minor
Humerus bone

FINISH

START

Execution

1. Stand sideways alongside a cable pulley adjusted to waist height, and grasp the handle with your outside hand, thumb pointing up.
2. With your elbow held firmly against your waist, move the handle in an outward arc away from your body, keeping your forearm parallel to the floor.
3. Slowly return the handle to the start position in front of your navel.

Muscles Involved

Primary: Infraspinatus, teres minor.

Secondary: Rear deltoid.

Anatomic Focus

Trajectory: During this movement, external rotation occurs at the shoulder joint from the combined action of the infraspinatus and the teres minor. Your hand moves in a horizontal arc with the forearm parallel to the floor. The upper arm is vertical, and your elbow is tight against your side.

Range: Your hand moves through an arc of approximately 90 degrees, like the hand of a clock moving between 10 and 2 o'clock.

Resistance: You cannot perform this exercise with a dumbbell while standing upright, because gravity does not provide resistance for the rotator cuff.

VARIATIONS

Dumbbell External Rotation

Lie across a flat exercise bench resting on your upper back, keeping your elbow in contact with the bench. Begin with your forearm vertically upward then lower the dumbbell down in a forward arc toward your waist until your forearm is parallel to the floor.

Additional variation:

Lying dumbbell external rotation: Lie side-down on a flat exercise bench while holding a dumbbell in your upper hand.

Internal Rotation

Scapula bone

Subscapularis

Humerus bone

START

FINISH

Execution

1. Stand sideways alongside a cable pulley adjusted to waist height, and grasp the handle with your inside hand, thumb pointing up.
2. With your elbow held firm against your waist, pull the handle inward across the front of your body, keeping your forearm parallel to the floor.
3. Slowly return the handle back to the start position.

Muscles Involved

Primary: Subscapularis.

Secondary: Pectoralis major.

Anatomic Focus

Trajectory: During this movement, the action of the subscapularis causes internal rotation at the shoulder joint. Your hand moves through a horizontal arc across the front of your torso, and the forearm remains parallel to the floor. The elbow and upper arm are held tight against the side of your body.

Range: Your hand moves through a 90-degree arc, like the hands of a clock moving between 10 and 2 o'clock.

Resistance: You cannot perform this exercise with a dumbbell while standing upright, because gravity does not provide resistance for the rotator cuff.

VARIATION

Dumbbell Internal Rotation

Lie across a flat exercise bench, resting on your upper back with your elbow in contact with the bench. Begin with your forearm out to the side, almost parallel to the floor, and then raise the dumbbell in a forward arc toward vertical.

Incline Side Raise

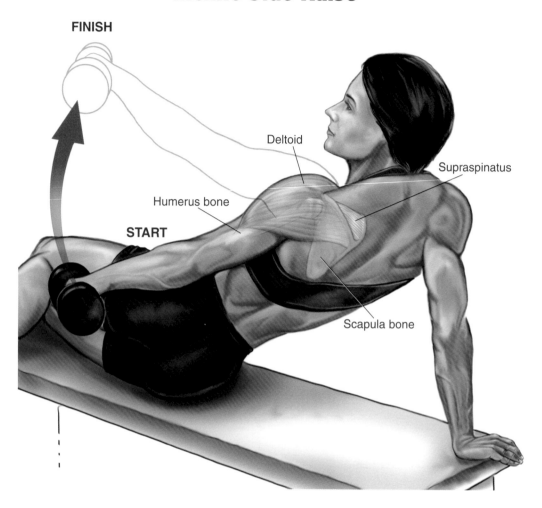

FINISH

Deltoid

Supraspinatus

Humerus bone

START

Scapula bone

Execution

1. Lie sideways on a bench with your torso inclined at 45 degrees supported by your underside arm.
2. With an overhand grip, raise the dumbbell upward to head height, keeping the elbow stiff.
3. Lower the weight back down to waist level.

Muscles Involved

Primary: Supraspinatus.

Secondary: Lateral deltoid, anterior deltoid.

Anatomic Focus

Range: The supraspinatus initiates the arm raise, acting as the primary muscle during the first 15 to 20 degrees of abduction. Gravity on the dumbbell in the inclined position causes resistance to be highest during the early phase of the inclined raise, focusing effort on the supraspinatus.

Trajectory: The supraspinatus is best isolated when the dumbbell is raised from in front of the hips.

Grip: A pronated grip (palm down) works best.

VARIATIONS

Cable Lateral Raise

This exercise is described on page 16. The supraspinatus initiates the arm raise and is active during the first 60 degrees of the movement. To focus on the rotator cuff muscle, terminate the upward phase when your hand reaches chest level.

Additional variation:

Dumbbell lateral raise: This exercise is described on page 14.

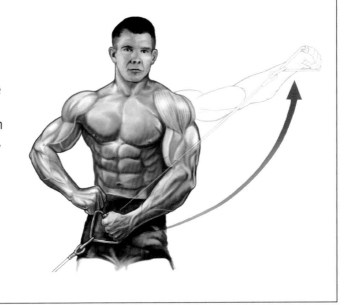

CHEST

The pectoralis major is a fan-shaped muscle that has two anatomic sections, or heads. The upper clavicular head arises from the clavicle (collarbone), and the lower sternal head arises from the sternum (breastbone). The two heads pass outward across the chest wall and merge into a single tendon that attaches to the humerus bone in the upper arm. As the muscle inserts, the tendon twists so that the upper head attaches beneath the lower head. When the pectoralis muscle contracts, movement takes place at the shoulder joint. Pectoralis major adducts, flexes, and internally rotates the arm, thus moving the arm forward and across the chest during movements such as a push-up or a bear hug. Even though the muscle has only two anatomic divisions, functionally it may be considered as having three sections (upper, middle, and lower), depending on the angle through which the arm is moved. As the position of the shoulder joint changes, certain fibers of the chest muscle have a better mechanical advantage to create motion. Other fibers of the chest muscle are still active but are not able to contract as much because of the shoulder position.

The side wall of the chest is formed by the serratus anterior. This muscle arises from the scapula behind, and it passes forward around the chest wall to attach to the upper eight ribs. The serrated edge of this muscle emerges from beneath the outer margin of the pectoralis muscle. The serratus anterior pulls (protracts) the scapula forward, stabilizing it against the rib cage. The serratus anterior is active during most chest exercises and works especially hard during the lockout phase of a push-up or bench press. The pectoralis minor muscle lies deep beneath the pectoralis major and is not visible. It has only a minor function and does not contribute to the size of the chest.

Anatomy of the Pectoralis Major

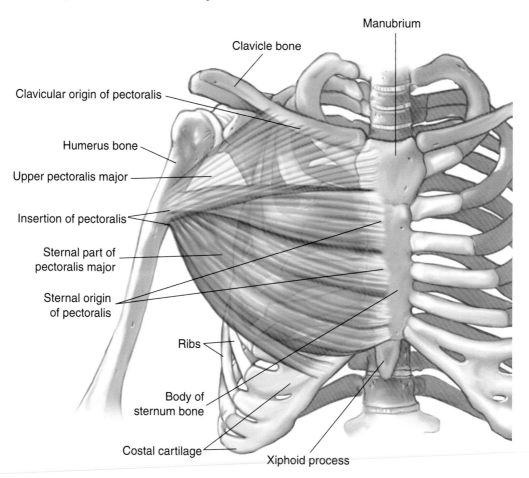

Chest Anatomy, Deep Muscles

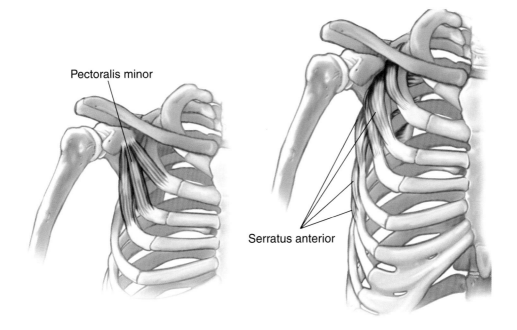

Pectoralis minor

Serratus anterior

Incline Barbell Press

FINISH

START

Upper pectoralis major
(clavicular head)

Anterior
deltoid

Triceps

Lower
pectoralis major

Execution

1. While seated on an incline bench, take a shoulder-width overhand grip on the bar.
2. Lower the weight slowly until the bar touches your upper chest.
3. Push the bar straight up until your elbows lock out.

Muscles Involved

Primary: Upper pectoralis major.

Secondary: Anterior deltoid, triceps.

Anatomic Focus

Trajectory: The angle of incline determines trajectory. As the backrest is raised up and the incline increases, the focus shifts progressively higher up the pectoral muscle. The upper pectoral is best targeted when the backrest is inclined at 30 to 45 degrees to the floor. Steeper inclines of 60 degrees or more switch the focus to the anterior deltoid.

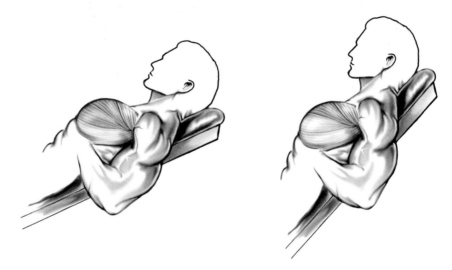

Increased incline shifts focus to higher up the pectoral muscle.

Hand spacing: A shoulder-width grip or slightly wider targets all areas of the upper pectoral muscle. Narrow hand spacing emphasizes the inner central portion of the chest and requires more effort from the triceps. Wider grips provide a greater stretch, targeting the outer portion of the muscle, and minimize triceps contribution; but as the hand spacing increases, so does the risk of injury.

Range of motion: To maximize pectoral work, flare your elbows out wide as the barbell is lowered. A shorter rep terminating the press just before lockout keeps tension on the pectorals and reduces triceps assistance.

VARIATION

Machine incline press: This provides better stability and safety than the standard barbell press. Many machines offer a choice of grips. A neutral grip (thumbs up, palms facing together) emphasizes the pectorals better than a pronated grip (palms forward).

Incline Dumbbell Press

FINISH

Anterior deltoid

START

Triceps

Upper pectoralis major
(clavicular head)

Pectoralis major, sternal part

Execution

1. While seated on an incline bench, start with the dumbbells at chest level, palms facing forward.
2. Press dumbbells vertically upward until elbows lock out.
3. Lower dumbbells back down to your upper chest.

Muscles Involved

Primary: Upper pectoralis major.

Secondary: Anterior deltoid, triceps.

Anatomic Focus

Trajectory: The angle of incline determines trajectory. As the backrest is raised up and the incline increases, the focus shifts progressively higher up the pectoral muscle. The upper pectoral is best targeted when the backrest is inclined at 30 to 45 degrees to the floor. Steeper inclines of 60 degrees or more switch the focus to the anterior deltoid.

Grip: Dumbbell orientation affects hand position. Grasping the dumbbells with a pronated grip (palms facing forward) affords a greater stretch as the weight is lowered to the start position. A neutral grip (palms facing together) generates a better contraction at the lockout position.

Neutral grip at lockout

Range of motion: To maximize pectoral work, flare your elbows out wide as the dumbbells are lowered, and touch the dumbbells together at the top. A shorter rep terminating the press just before lockout keeps tension on the pectorals. The lower the dumbbells descend, the more the chest muscle stretches. Lowering the dumbbells too far can cause shoulder injury; it is safer to terminate the descent when the dumbbells reach chest level.

VARIATION

Variable-grip dumbbell press: Begin the exercise by holding the dumbbells with a pronated grip (palms forward), and rotate the dumbbells during the press so your palms face together (neutral grip) at lockout.

Incline Dumbbell Fly

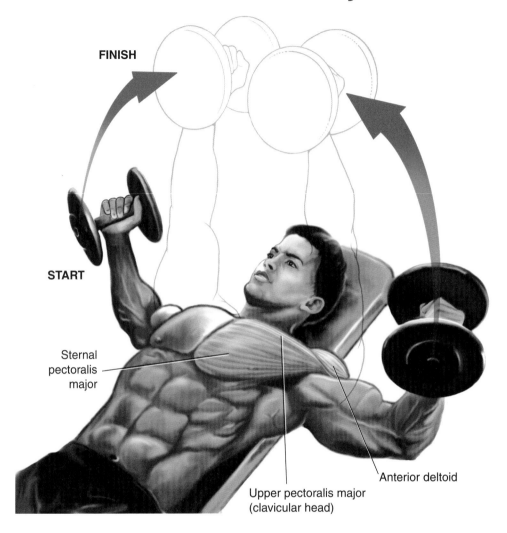

FINISH

START

Sternal pectoralis major

Upper pectoralis major (clavicular head)

Anterior deltoid

Execution

1. While seated on an incline bench, begin with dumbbells directly above your chest, palms facing together.
2. Lower the dumbbells outward, bending elbows slightly as weight descends to chest level.
3. Raise dumbbells back up and together.

Muscles Involved

Primary: Upper pectoralis major.

Secondary: Anterior deltoid.

Anatomic Focus

Trajectory: The angle of incline determines trajectory. As the backrest is raised up and the incline increases, the focus shifts progressively higher up the pectoral muscle. The upper pectoral is best targeted when the backrest is inclined at 30 to 45 degrees to the floor.

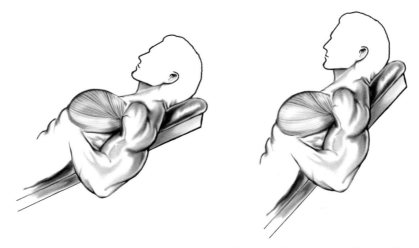

Increased incline shifts focus to higher up the pectoral muscle.

Grip: Dumbbell orientation affects hand position. The fly exercise works best when the dumbbells are held with a neutral grip (palms facing together), but a pronated grip (palms facing forward) can also be used as a variation.

Range of motion: The lower the dumbbells descend, the greater the pectoral stretch. Too much stretch can cause injury to the muscle and the shoulder joint. It's safer to terminate the descent when the dumbbells reach chest level.

VARIATION

Machine fly: Performing the machine fly (described on page 54) with the seat low and the handles at eye level will target the upper pectorals.

Low-Pulley Cable Fly

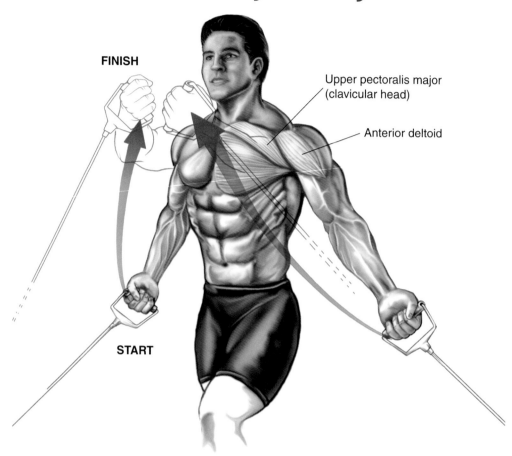

FINISH

Upper pectoralis major
(clavicular head)

Anterior deltoid

START

Execution

1. In each hand, grasp a D-handle attached to the low pulleys, and stand upright.
2. Raise your hands up in a forward arc until the handles meet at head height.
3. Keeping your elbows stiff, lower the handles back to the start position.

Muscles Involved

Primary: Upper pectoralis major.

Secondary: Anterior deltoid.

Anatomic Focus

Trajectory: Standing forward so that the pulleys are slightly behind you affords a better trajectory to target the pectoral muscles.

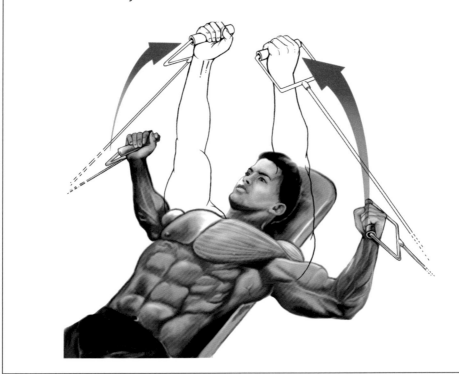

Incline Cable Fly

Perform this exercise while lying on an incline exercise bench positioned centrally between the low pulleys, using similar technique to that of the incline dumbbell fly (described earlier).

Barbell Bench Press

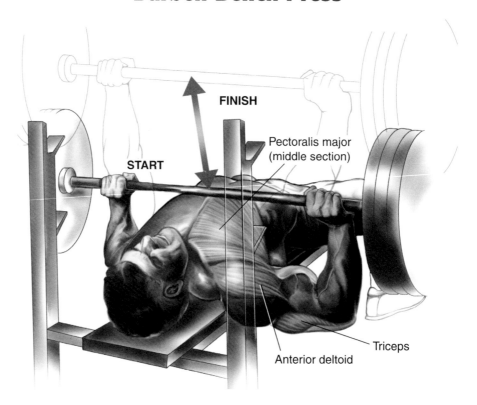

FINISH

Pectoralis major
(middle section)

START

Triceps

Anterior deltoid

Execution

1. While lying on a flat bench, take a shoulder-width overhand grip on the bar.
2. Lower the weight slowly down to touch the middle chest.
3. Push the bar straight up until your elbows lock out.

Muscles Involved

Primary: Pectoralis major.

Secondary: Anterior deltoid, triceps.

Anatomic Focus

Body position: Your torso should lie flat with your shoulders and buttocks in contact with the bench. Plant your feet firmly on the floor for stability. If your lower back is arched (or your buttocks rise off the bench), the focus shifts to the lower pectorals. Raising your feet off the floor by bending your knees may help target the middle chest, but stability and balance are compromised when your feet are not in contact with the floor.

Hand spacing: The ideal hand spacing is shoulder width or slightly wider. A narrow (close) grip emphasizes the inner pectorals and also targets the triceps. Wider grips target the outer section of the muscle and minimize triceps contribution.

Narrow grip　　　　　　　**Wide grip**

Trajectory: The bar should move vertically up and down from the middle chest (nipple area). Flare your elbows out as the bar is lowered to maximize pectoral isolation.

Range of motion: A shorter rep terminating the press just before lockout keeps tension on the pectorals and reduces the amount of triceps assistance.

Grip: An underhand (supinated) grip on the bar switches the focus to the triceps.

VARIATIONS

Machine Chest Press

Machines provide better stability and safety than the standard barbell press. Many machines offer a choice of grips. A neutral grip (thumbs up, palms facing together) isolates the pectorals better than a pronated grip (palms forward).

Additional variation:

Close-grip bench press: Perform the exercise with hands spaced approximately 6 inches (15 cm) apart. The narrow grip targets the inner pecs and works the triceps.

Dumbbell Bench Press

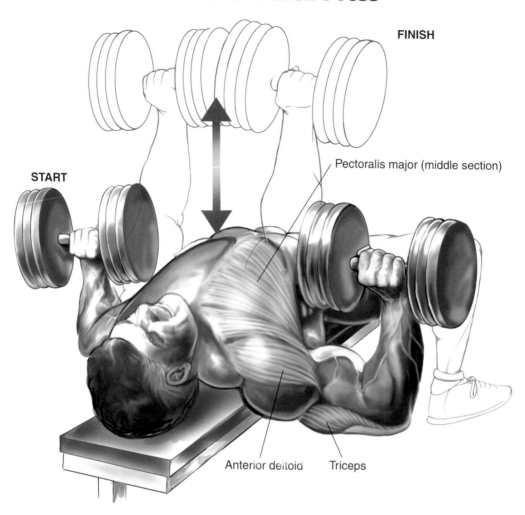

FINISH

START

Pectoralis major (middle section)

Anterior deltoid   Triceps

Execution

1. While lying on a flat bench, start with the dumbbells at chest level, palms facing forward.
2. Press dumbbells vertically upward until elbows lock out.
3. Lower dumbbells back down to middle chest.

Muscles Involved

Primary: Pectoralis major.

Secondary: Anterior deltoid, triceps.

Anatomic Focus

Grip: Dumbbell orientation affects hand position. Holding the dumbbells with palms facing forward (pronated grip) provides more stretch as the weight is lowered to the start position. Holding the dumbbells with palms facing together (neutral grip) allows a better contraction in the lockout position.

Neutral grip at lockout

Trajectory: Your torso should lie flat on the bench, and the dumbbells should move vertically up and down from the middle chest (nipple area). To maximize pectoral isolation, flare your elbows out wide during descent and touch the dumbbells together at lockout.

Range of motion: A shorter rep terminating the press just before lockout keeps tension on the pectorals and reduces triceps assistance. The lower the dumbbells descend, the more the chest muscle stretches. Lowering the dumbbells too far can cause shoulder injury; it is safer to terminate the descent when the dumbbells reach chest level.

VARIATION

Variable-grip dumbbell press: Hold the dumbbells with a pronated grip (palms forward) at the start; rotate the dumbbells as you press so that palms face together (neutral grip) at lockout.

Dumbbell Fly

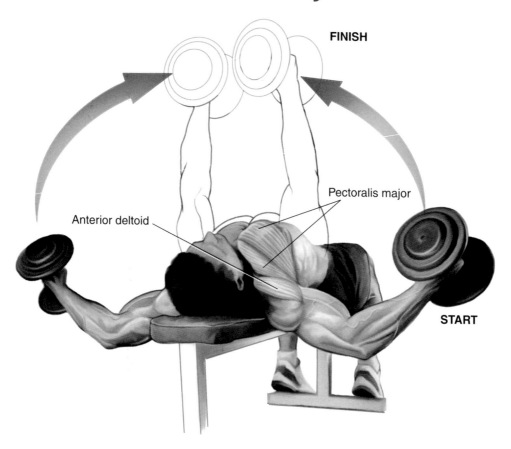

FINISH

Pectoralis major

Anterior deltoid

START

Execution

1. While lying on a flat bench, begin with dumbbells directly above middle chest, palms facing together.
2. Lower the dumbbells out wide, bending elbows slightly as weight descends to chest level.
3. Raise dumbbells together in an upward arc back to the vertical position.

Muscles Involved

Primary: Pectoralis major.

Secondary: Anterior deltoid.

Anatomic Focus

Grip: Dumbbell orientation affects hand position. The fly exercise works best when the dumbbells are held with a neutral grip (palms facing together), but a pronated grip (palms facing forward) can also be used for variation.

Range of motion: The lower the dumbbells descend, the greater the pectoral stretch, but also the greater the chance of injury. It's safer to terminate the descent when the dumbbells reach chest level.

VARIATION

Cable Fly

Perform this exercise with the exercise bench positioned centrally between two cable machines, and use D-handles attached to the low pulleys.

Machine Fly

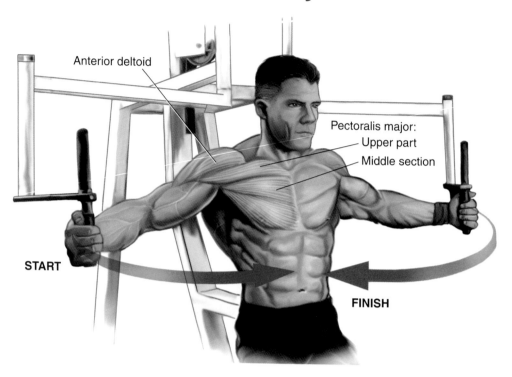

Anterior deltoid

Pectoralis major:
Upper part
Middle section

START

FINISH

Execution

1. Grab the vertical handles, elbows slightly bent.
2. Squeeze the handles together until they touch in front of your chest.
3. Let your hands move back to the start position, keeping your elbows up.

Muscles Involved

Primary: Pectoralis major.

Secondary: Anterior deltoid.

Anatomic Focus

Grip: The fly exercise works best with a neutral grip (palms facing together), but a pronated grip (palms facing forward) can also be used for variation. Keep your elbows stiff and slightly bent throughout the movement.

Range of motion: The inner central portion of the pectoral muscle does most of the work as the handles are squeezed together. To emphasize the inner pecs, use a narrow range of motion focusing on the squeeze position. Perform partial reps, in which your hands move through a short 45-degree arc from the 12 o'clock (handles touching) position outward to 10 o'clock on the left and 2 o'clock on the right side. Keep your elbows straight to achieve maximum squeeze. The emphasis switches to the outer pecs when your hands move out wide. Do not allow the handles to pass behind the plane of your body, or you will enter the injury zone. It's safer to terminate the stretch phase when your arms are in line with your chest.

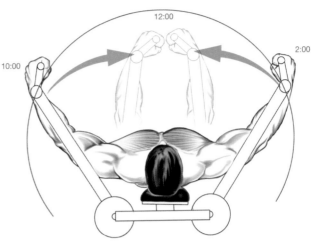

Partial reps target the inner pectorals.

Trajectory: Position the seat so the handles are level with your chest. To maximize pectoral isolation, keep your elbows high (shoulder level) during the movement.

Body position: When the seat is low and the handles are held high, the upper chest is emphasized. When the seat is high and the handles are held low, the lower chest is emphasized.

Resistance: Unlike dumbbell flys, where the resistance varies during the lift, the machine fly affords a uniform resistance throughout the motion and is an excellent exercise for targeting the inner pecs.

VARIATIONS

Pec-Deck Fly

The pec-deck fly is a similar exercise using elbow pads instead of handles.

Additional variation:

One-arm machine fly: You can do this exercise using one arm at a time.

Decline Press

FINISH

Lower pectoralis major

START

Anterior deltoid

Triceps

Execution

1. Lie on a decline bench and take a shoulder-width overhand grip on the bar.
2. Lower the weight slowly down to touch your lower chest.
3. Push the bar straight up until your elbows lock out.

Muscles Involved

Primary: Lower pectoralis major (sternal head).

Secondary: Triceps, anterior deltoid.

Anatomic Focus

Trajectory: The decline angle determines trajectory. As the bench is tilted head-down and the decline gets steeper, the focus shifts progressively lower down the pectoral muscle. The lower pectoral is best targeted at a decline of 20 to 40 degrees to the floor. Steeper declines shift the focus from the chest to the triceps. Flare your elbows out as the bar is lowered to maximize pectoral isolation.

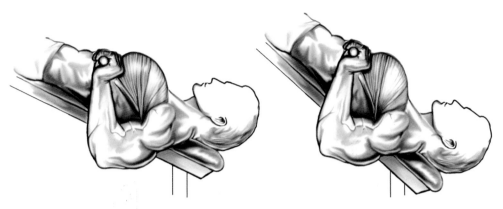

Increased decline shifts focus to lower down the pectoral muscle.

Hand spacing: The ideal hand spacing is shoulder width. Wider grips target the outer section of the muscle, afford a greater stretch, and minimize triceps contribution. A narrow (close) grip targets the inner pectorals and requires more work from the triceps.

Range of motion: A shorter rep terminating the press just before lockout keeps tension on the pectorals and reduces the amount of triceps assistance.

VARIATIONS

Decline Dumbbell Press

Performing the decline press using two dumbbells affords an increased range of motion as the weight is lowered. A barbell stops when it touches the chest, whereas dumbbells can be lowered farther for additional stretch at the bottom of the lift.

Additional variation:

Machine decline press:
Performing the decline press on a machine, such as the Smith machine, affords better stability and safety.

Decline Dumbbell Fly

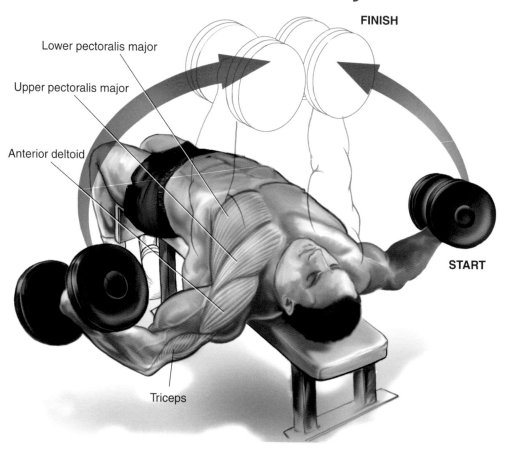

FINISH

Lower pectoralis major

Upper pectoralis major

Anterior deltoid

START

Triceps

Execution

1. While lying on a decline bench, begin with dumbbells directly above your chest, palms facing together.
2. Lower the dumbbells outward, bending elbows slightly as weight descends to chest level.
3. Raise dumbbells back up and together.

Muscles Involved

Primary: Lower pectoralis major (sternal head)

Secondary: Anterior deltoid, triceps.

Anatomic Focus

Trajectory: The decline angle determines trajectory. As the bench is tilted head-down and the decline gets steeper, the focus shifts progressively lower down the pectoral muscle. The lower pectoral is best targeted at a decline of 20 to 40 degrees to the floor.

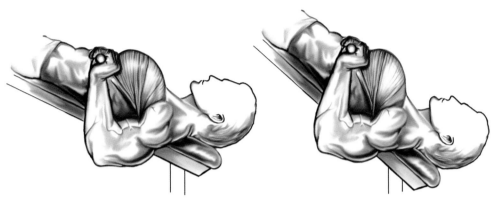

Increased decline shifts focus to lower down the pectoral muscle.

Grip: Dumbbell orientation affects hand position. The fly exercise works best when the dumbbells are held with a neutral grip (palms facing together), but a pronated grip (palms facing forward) can also be used as a variation.

Range of motion: The lower the dumbbells descend, the greater the pectoral stretch, but also the greater the chance of injury. It's safer to terminate the descent when the dumbbells reach chest level.

VARIATION

Variable-grip dumbbell fly: As the weight is lowered, hold the dumbbells with a pronated grip (palms forward) at the bottom, and then rotate the dumbbells during the lift so your palms face together (neutral grip) at the top.

Cable Crossover

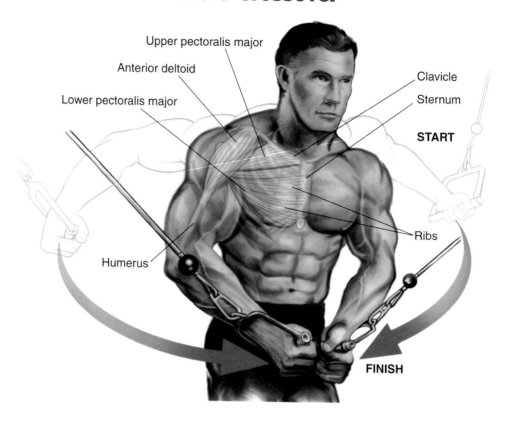

Upper pectoralis major

Anterior deltoid

Lower pectoralis major

Clavicle

Sternum

START

Ribs

Humerus

FINISH

Execution

1. Standing upright, grasp the D-handles attached to the high pulleys of a cable machine.
2. Squeeze the handles down together until your hands touch in front of your waist; keep elbows slightly bent.
3. Slowly return to the start position with your hands at shoulder level.

Muscles Involved

Primary: Lower pectoralis major (sternal head).

Secondary: Anterior deltoid, triceps.

Anatomic Focus

Trajectory: Your torso should be upright or tilted forward slightly at the waist. The level at which your hands meet determines the focus on the muscle. A low trajectory, in which the handles meet in front of your hips or waist, targets the lowest fibers of the pectoral muscle. A high trajectory, in which the handles meet at chest level, targets the midsection of the pecs.

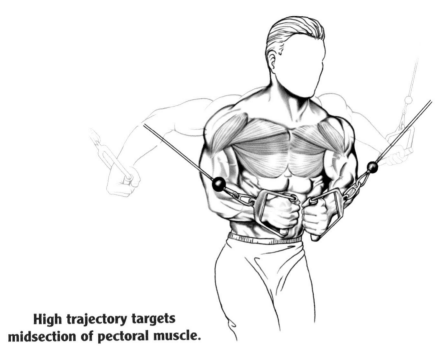

High trajectory targets midsection of pectoral muscle.

Range of motion: Crossing over your hands at the bottom increases the range of motion and targets the inner, central portion of the pectorals. Extending the start position by allowing your hands to pass above shoulder or head height affords a greater stretch but also places unnecessary stress on the shoulder joint.

VARIATION

Seated crossover: Newer machines allow you to perform this exercise while seated with a back support.

Chest Dip

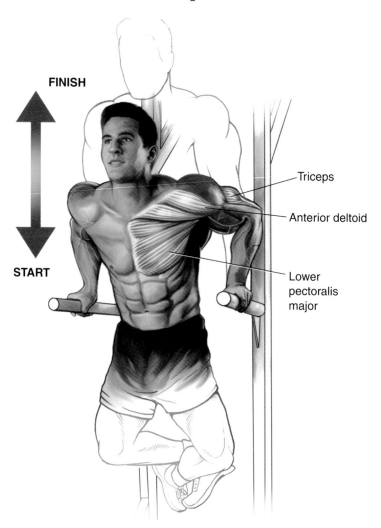

FINISH

START

Triceps

Anterior deltoid

Lower
pectoralis
major

Execution

1. Grab the parallel bars, supporting your body with elbows locked straight.
2. Bend your elbows, lowering your torso until upper arms are parallel to the floor.
3. Push yourself back up until your elbows lock out.

Muscles Involved

Primary: Lower pectoralis major (sternal head).

Secondary: Triceps, anterior deltoid.

Anatomic Focus

Trajectory: The position of your torso affects the focus of the exercise. A slight forward tilt is better for targeting the pectorals, and the more you bend forward the harder you work the pectorals. An upright posture shifts the focus to the triceps, and the more you straighten your torso the more you involve the triceps. Flare your elbows out as you descend to maximize pectoral isolation.

Grip: A standard grip on the parallel bars with thumbs pointing forward works best when targeting the chest. A reverse grip with thumbs pointing backward shifts the focus to the triceps.

Tilting forward targets the pectorals.

VARIATION

Machine dip: You can perform this exercise while seated on a machine. But since most dip machines restrict torso motion, they tend to target the triceps more than the chest.

Anatomically, the rear torso (back) consists of several layers of muscle, stacked like a sandwich. Functionally, and for bodybuilding purposes, the back is best considered in three sections, resembling triangular segments of a quilted blanket.

The upper back is made up of a large triangular-shaped muscle called the trapezius. It originates along the upper spine from the skull down to the last rib (that is, all the cervical and thoracic vertebrae). The upper fibers of the trapezius (in the neck) attach to the outer tip of the shoulder on the clavicle, acromion, and scapula. The middle and lower fibers of the trapezius (in the upper back) attach to the scapula (shoulder blade). The upper traps elevate the scapula to shrug the shoulders and rotate the scapula to assist shoulder abduction. The middle traps retract the scapula, pulling the shoulders backward; the lower traps depress the scapula downward.

Underneath the trapezius are three muscles that anchor the scapula to the spine: the levator scapulae, rhomboid major, and rhomboid minor. The levator scapulae muscles assist the upper traps to elevate the scapula. The rhomboid muscles work with the middle traps to retract the scapula. These scapular retractor muscles lie under the trapezius and add muscular thickness to the upper back.

The middle back consists of the latissimus dorsi, a large fan-shaped muscle that arises from the lower half of the spinal column and the rear ridge of the pelvic bone (posterior iliac crest). From its large origin, the latissimus converges into a bandlike tendon that attaches to the upper humerus (next to the tendon of the pectoralis major). When the latissimus dorsi contracts, movement takes place at the shoulder joint. The latissimus dorsi pulls the upper arm downward and backward (shoulder extension); hence this muscle is targeted by pulldowns, pull-ups, and rows. The latissimus also pulls the arm in against the side of the body (adduction).

The lower back is made up of the erector spinae (or sacrospinalis) muscles that run alongside the entire length of the spinal column. In the lumbar region, the erector spinae split into three columns: the iliocostalis, longissimus, and spinalis. These muscles are the pillars of strength in the lower back that stabilize the spine and extend the torso, arching the spine backward.

The trapezius and latissimus dorsi are concerned primarily with movements of the shoulder and arm. It is the sacrospinalis muscles that cause movements of the spine and torso. Exercises that target the back muscles include shrugs, pulldowns, pull-ups, rows, and lumbar extensions. The deadlift is a compound, multijoint exercise that utilizes *all* of the back muscles (see page 88).

Anatomy of the Back Muscles

Superficial muscles

Deep muscles

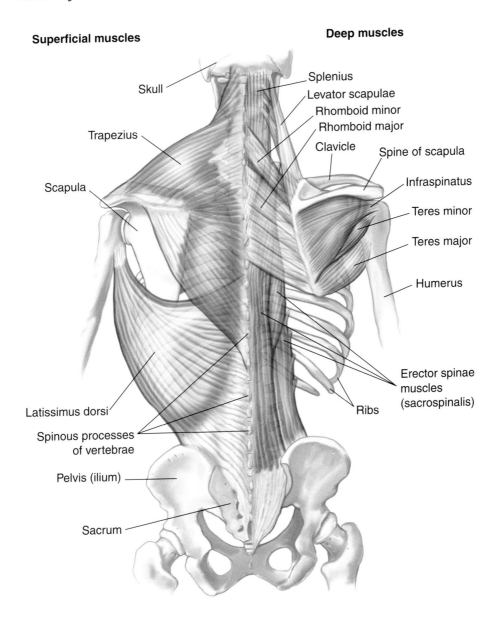

Skull

Trapezius

Scapula

Splenius

Levator scapulae

Rhomboid minor

Rhomboid major

Clavicle

Spine of scapula

Infraspinatus

Teres minor

Teres major

Humerus

Erector spinae muscles (sacrospinalis)

Ribs

Latissimus dorsi

Spinous processes of vertebrae

Pelvis (ilium)

Sacrum

Barbell Shrug

Upper part of trapezius

Deltoid

FINISH

START

Execution

1. Hold a barbell at arms' length in front of the thighs, using an overhand shoulder-width grip.
2. Keeping arms stiff, shrug your shoulders as high as possible, pulling the bar vertically upward.
3. Lower the bar slowly down to the start position, stretching the trapezius.

Muscles Involved

Primary: Trapezius (upper and middle fibers).

Secondary: Levator scapulae, deltoid, erector spinae, forearms.

Anatomic Focus

Hand spacing: A shoulder-width or narrower grip on the bar emphasizes the trapezius. A wider grip works the deltoid as well.

Trajectory: Lift the bar straight up and down. Do not roll or rotate the shoulders.

Body position: Performing the shrug while standing vertically upright hits the muscle centrally. Tilting the torso slightly backward at the waist targets the upper trapezius in the neck, whereas leaning slightly forward hits the midsection of the muscle behind the shoulders.

Range of motion: The higher the bar is raised, the harder the trapezius works.

VARIATIONS

Rear Shrug

Performing the exercise with the barbell behind your hips causes scapular retraction, pulling the shoulders backward to emphasize the middle fibers of the trapezius.

Additional variation:

Machine shrug: This affords a choice of grips—pronated (thumbs pointing in) and neutral (thumbs pointing forward). A neutral grip (thumbs pointing forward) emphasizes the upper trapezius in the neck, whereas a pronated grip (thumbs pointing in) targets the middle trapezius in the back.

Dumbbell Shrug

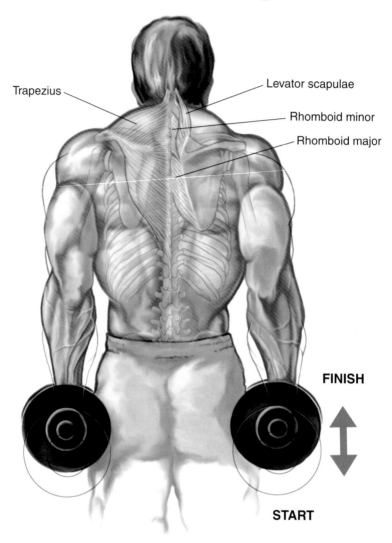

Trapezius

Levator scapulae

Rhomboid minor

Rhomboid major

FINISH

START

Execution

1. Stand upright with a dumbbell in each hand, hands hanging at your sides.
2. Keeping arms straight, shrug your shoulders upward as high as possible.
3. Lower the dumbbells back down.

Muscles Involved

Primary: Trapezius (upper and middle fibers).

Secondary: Levator scapulae, deltoid, erector spinae, forearms.

Anatomic Focus

Grip: A neutral grip (thumbs pointing forward) emphasizes the upper trapezius in the neck, whereas a pronated grip (thumbs pointing in) targets the middle trapezius in the back.

Body position: Tilting your torso slightly backward at the waist targets the upper trapezius, whereas leaning slightly forward hits the muscle lower down the neck. Performing the shrug while standing vertically upright hits the upper and middle sections of the trapezius muscle.

Range of motion: The higher the weight is raised, the harder the trapezius works. The farther the dumbbells are lowered, the greater the stretch at the bottom.

VARIATION

Retracting Shrug

Begin with the dumbbells in front, using a pronated grip. Squeeze shoulder blades together during the shrug, finishing with the dumbbells at your sides in a neutral grip. The dumbbells are lifted upward (scapular elevation), working the upper traps, and backward (scapular retraction), working the middle section of the trapezius.

Barbell Upright Row

Deltoid

Trapezius

FINISH

Scapula

START

Execution

1. Hold a barbell at arms' length, using an overhand shoulder-width grip.
2. Pull the bar vertically upward until it reaches your chin, raising the elbows as high as possible.
3. Lower the bar slowly down to the arms' extended position.

Muscles Involved

Primary: Trapezius, deltoid.

Secondary: Levator scapulae, erector spinae, forearms.

Anatomic Focus

Hand spacing: A shoulder-width or narrower grip on the bar emphasizes the trapezius. A wider grip works the deltoid as well.

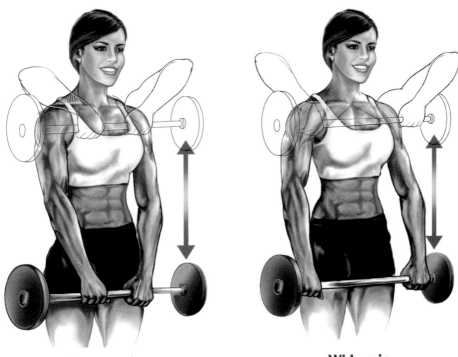

Narrow grip   **Wide grip**

Body position: Performing the row while standing vertically upright hits the trapezius centrally. Tilting your torso slightly backward at the waist targets the upper trapezius, whereas leaning slightly forward hits the muscle lower down the neck.

Trajectory: To emphasize the trapezius (not the deltoid), raise the bar close to your body during the exercise.

Range of motion: The higher the bar is raised, the harder the trapezius works but the greater the risk of shoulder-impingement pain.

VARIATIONS

Cable upright row: Using a straight bar attached to the low pulley of a cable machine provides a steady resistance throughout the movement.

Machine upright row: Using a Smith machine provides a single plane of vertical motion that may help focus your effort.

Seated Cable Row

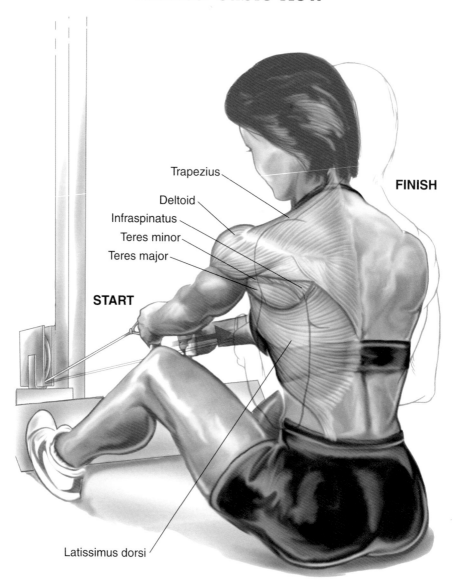

Trapezius

Deltoid

Infraspinatus

Teres minor

Teres major

START

FINISH

Latissimus dorsi

Execution

1. Grab the handles with arms extended in front.
2. Pull the handles high toward your chest, keeping your spine straight.
3. Return the handles to the start position.

Muscles Involved

Primary: Trapezius (middle and lower fibers), latissimus dorsi.
Secondary: Rhomboids, rear deltoid.

Anatomic Focus

Hand spacing: Spacing your hands farther apart will target the outer trapezius, whereas placing your hands closer together will focus on the inner portion of the trapezius.

Grip: A pronated (overhand) grip tends to target the upper and middle trapezius, whereas a neutral (thumbs up) grip hits the middle and lower trapezius. A supinated (underhand) grip switches the focus to the latissimus dorsi.

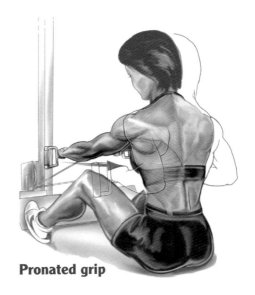

Pronated grip

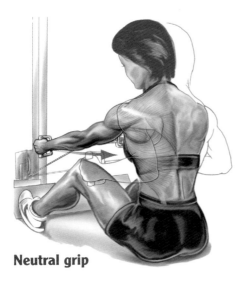

Neutral grip

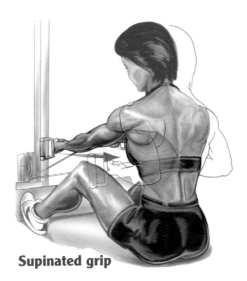

Supinated grip

Trajectory: To target the trapezius, pull the handles or bar through a high trajectory toward the chest; a low trajectory toward the abdomen works the latissimus dorsi.

Body position: Keep your back straight and torso upright.

Range of motion: Pull your elbows back and high as far as possible, and squeeze the shoulder blades together to maximize muscle contraction.

VARIATION

Machine row: See description of this exercise on page 84.

Wide-Grip Pulldown

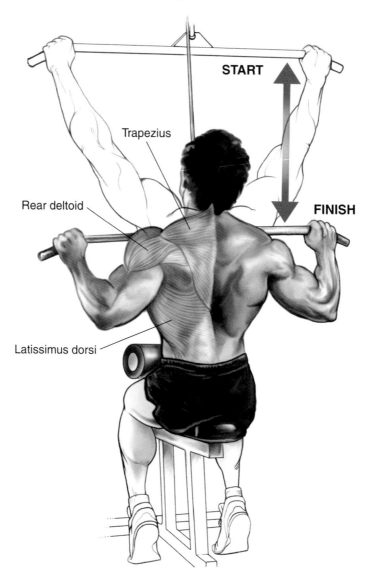

START

FINISH

Trapezius

Rear deltoid

Latissimus dorsi

Execution

1. Take an overhand grip on the bar with hands 6 inches (15 cm) wider than shoulder width.
2. Pull the bar down to the upper chest, squeezing your lats.
3. Return the bar to the start position overhead.

Muscles Involved

Primary: Latissimus dorsi (outer section).

Secondary: Rear deltoid, lower trapezius, rhomboids.

Anatomic Focus

Hand spacing: As the hand spacing gets wider, the focus shifts to the outermost section of the latissimus dorsi under the armpit. This portion of the muscle creates width across the back.

Grip: An overhand (pronated) grip works best for the wide-grip pulldown. Grasping the angled section at the outer edges of the handlebar affords a better contraction in the lats.

Trajectory: When your torso is upright, the bar is pulled vertically downward using shoulder adduction, which emphasizes the outer lats. Leaning your torso back about 30 degrees from the vertical plane creates a trajectory that uses shoulder extension, which emphasizes the inner lower lats.

Range of motion: To maximize range of motion, stretch the lats at the top position, and squeeze the lats at the bottom by pulling the elbows down and back as far as possible.

VARIATIONS

Wide-Grip Pull-Up

Pull-ups are similar to pulldowns, except that resistance is provided by your own body weight. Pull-ups primarily use shoulder adduction and therefore tend to work the outer lats, generating width across the back.

Additional variations:

Handlebar variations: The angled ends of a wide-grip pulldown bar offer several advantages over a straight bar: improved trajectory, less stress through the wrist joint, and a few extra inches of motion before the bar touches the chest.

Behind-the-neck pulldown: Pulling the bar down behind the neck is a less favorable trajectory that can cause injury to the shoulder joint.

Close-Grip Pulldown

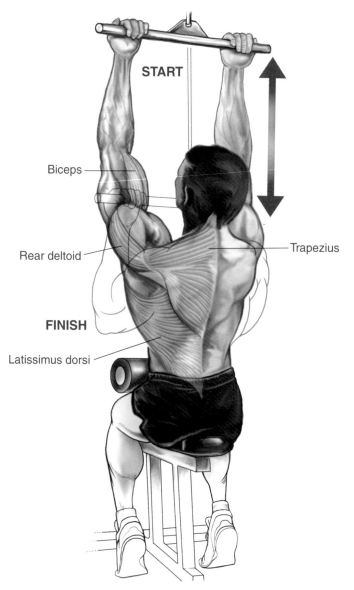

START

Biceps

Rear deltoid

Trapezius

FINISH

Latissimus dorsi

Execution

1. Take an underhand (reverse) grip on the bar, with hands spaced 6 to 12 inches (15 to 30 cm) apart.
2. Pull the bar down to the upper chest, squeezing your lats.
3. Return the bar to the start position, arms extended overhead.

Muscles Involved

Primary: Latissimus dorsi (inner section).

Secondary: Lower trapezius, rhomboids, rear deltoid, biceps.

Anatomic Focus

Hand spacing: As the hand spacing gets narrower, the focus shifts to the innermost section of the latissimus dorsi, generating thickness and depth in the middle back.

Grip: The close-grip pulldown uses shoulder extension rather than adduction. The arms are pulled down and backward, which emphasizes the inner lower sections of the lats.

Trajectory: Leaning your torso back about 30 degrees from the vertical plane improves trajectory and helps isolate the latissimus dorsi muscle. Do not lean back too far or pull the weight down with momentum.

Range of motion: Stretch the lats at the top, and squeeze the lats at the bottom by pulling the elbows down and back as far as possible.

VARIATIONS

Handlebar Variation

Handlebar attachments allow a neutral grip (palms facing together). This hand position is midway between a pronated (overhand) grip and a supinated (underhand) grip. An overhand grip targets the outer lats, an underhand grip isolates the inner lats, and a neutral grip hits the muscle centrally.

Additional variation:

Close-grip pull-up: Pull-ups are similar to pulldowns except that resistance provided by your own body weight is not easily adjusted.

Barbell Row

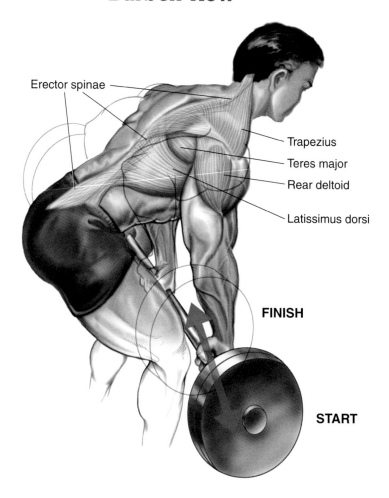

Erector spinae

Trapezius

Teres major

Rear deltoid

Latissimus dorsi

FINISH

START

Execution

1. Taking an overhand shoulder-width grip on the barbell, bend your torso forward at an angle of 45 degrees to the floor.
2. Pull the bar vertically upward to touch the lower chest, keeping your spine straight and knees slightly bent.
3. Lower the bar down to the arms' extended position.

Muscles Involved

Primary: Latissimus dorsi.

Secondary: Erector spinae, trapezius, rhomboids, rear deltoid.

Anatomic Focus

Hand spacing: Spacing your hands shoulder-width apart or closer targets the central inner section of the lats, whereas a wider grip targets the outer lats.

Grip: An underhand (supinated) grip on the bar facilitates a closer hand spacing, emphasizing shoulder extension and targeting the central inner section of the lats. A greater contribution from the biceps with an underhand grip provides added strength during the row.

Trajectory: Pulling the bar up higher toward the chest targets the upper latissimus and trapezius. Pulling the bar through a lower trajectory to touch the abdomen targets the lower lats.

Body position: Keep your spine straight. The lower back should never be rounded in an attempt to lower the bar farther, because this will provoke injury.

Supinated grip

VARIATION

T-Bar Row

This variation requires less effort to stabilize body position during the row, because one end of the bar pivots at a fixed point on the floor. Stand facing the loaded end with feet positioned on either side of the bar. With your spine straight and knees slightly bent, lift the loaded end using the T-bar attachment. Some row apparatus provide an inclined chest pad to support the torso and minimize load across the lower spine.

Dumbbell Row

Trapezius

Latissimus dorsi

Rear deltoid

Biceps

FINISH

START

Execution

1. Grasp a dumbbell with palm facing in. Rest the opposite hand and knee on a bench, keeping your spine straight and just above parallel to the floor.
2. Pull the dumbbell vertically upward alongside your torso, raising the elbow as high as possible.
3. Lower the dumbbell down to the start position.

Muscles Involved

Primary: Latissimus dorsi.

Secondary: Trapezius, rhomboids, rear deltoid, erector spinae, biceps.

Anatomic Focus

Grip: A neutral grip with the dumbbell parallel to the torso works best. The dumbbell will tend to jam against your torso if a pronated or supinated grip is attempted.

Trajectory: Pulling the dumbbell toward the chest works the upper latissimus and lower trapezius. Raising the dumbbell through a lower trajectory toward the abdomen targets the lower lats.

Range of motion: Maximize the range of motion by stretching the latissimus at the bottom and raising the elbow as high as possible at the top.

Body position: With your torso supported on the bench, stress through the spine is reduced.

VARIATION

One-Arm Seated Cable Row

Perform a seated low-pulley cable row by grabbing the handle with one hand at a time. Rowing one arm at a time allows the elbow to be pulled back farther, thereby maximizing muscle contraction in the lats.

Machine Row

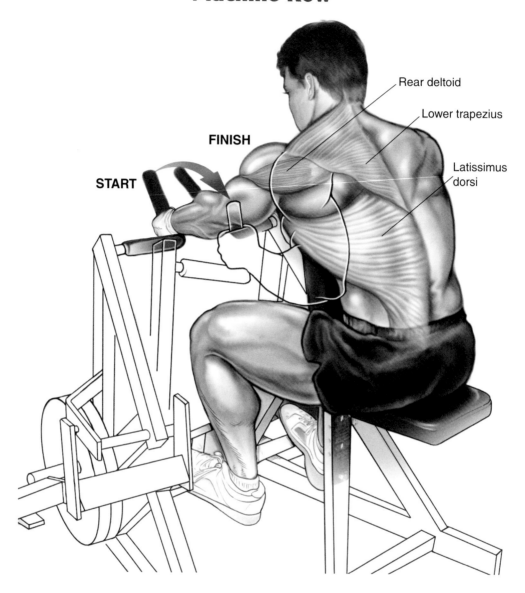

Rear deltoid

Lower trapezius

Latissimus dorsi

FINISH

START

Execution

1. Grab the handles with arms extended in front, supporting your torso against the chest pad.
2. Pull the handles toward your upper abdomen, keeping your spine straight.
3. Return the weight to the start position.

Muscles Involved

Primary: Latissimus dorsi.

Secondary: Trapezius, rhomboids, rear deltoid.

Anatomic Focus

Hand spacing: Spacing your hands farther apart will target the outer lats, whereas spacing your hands closer together will isolate the inner lats.

Grip: A pronated (overhand) grip tends to target the upper and outer lats, a neutral (thumbs up) grip hits the central section of the back, and a supinated (underhand) grip works the lower lats. As the grip changes from pronation to neutral to supination, the elbows move progressively closer to the sides of your body.

Pronated grip   **Neutral grip**   **Supinated grip**

Trajectory: Pulling the handle through a high trajectory toward the chest targets the upper latissimus and trapezius, whereas a lower trajectory toward the abdomen targets the lower lats. Adjust the seat height to change trajectory. Raising the seat creates a low trajectory, and lowering the seat provides a high trajectory.

Range of motion: Pull your elbows as far back as possible and squeeze the shoulder blades together to maximize muscle contraction.

Body position: With the torso supported against a chest pad, load across the spine is reduced.

VARIATION

Seated cable row: See description of this exercise on page 74.

Lumbar Extension

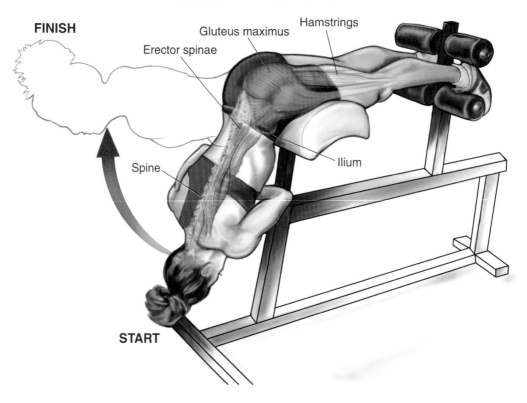

FINISH

Hamstrings

Gluteus maximus

Erector spinae

Spine

Ilium

START

Execution

1. Lie facedown with hips supported on the bench and ankles secured under the pads.
2. Begin with your torso hanging down, bent 90 degrees at the waist.
3. Raise your body up until your torso is just above parallel to the floor.

Muscles Involved

Primary: Erector spinae.

Secondary: Latissimus dorsi, gluteals, hamstrings.

Anatomic Focus

Hand position: Hands may be interlocked behind your lower back or folded across your chest.

Resistance: Add resistance by holding a weight plate against the front of your chest.

Trajectory: You can perform the movement at an incline angle (see Variations section).

Range of motion: Your torso should move up and down through an arc of about 90 degrees. Avoid hyperextending your spine. The erector muscles work to stabilize and straighten the spine, while the glutes and hamstrings generate hip extension during this movement.

VARIATIONS

Incline Lumbar Extension

Performing the movement at an incline with the hips supported high and the ankles closer to the floor makes the exercise easier. The disadvantage is that the inclined position shifts the focus away from the lumbar muscles onto the buttocks and hamstrings.

Incline lumbar extension

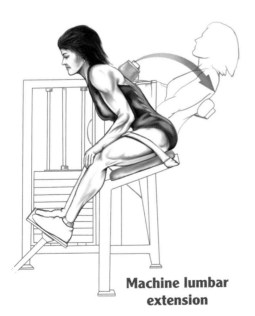

Machine lumbar extension

Machine Lumbar Extension

You can also perform the exercise while seated on a lumbar extension machine that provides variable resistance. To avoid injury, do not flex the spine too far forward or extend too far backward.

Deadlift

Splenius

Trapezius

Latissimus dorsi

FINISH

Erector spinae

Gluteus maximus

Hamstrings

START

Execution

1. Take a shoulder-width overhand grip on the barbell with arms extended, and squat down, bending the knees and hips.
2. Keeping your spine straight and elbows stiff, stand upright, lifting the bar upward to hip level.
3. Slowly lower the bar back to the floor.

Muscles Involved

Primary: Erector spinae, gluteals, hamstrings.

Secondary: Trapezius, latissimus dorsi, quadriceps, forearms.

Anatomic Focus

Hand spacing: Hands should be spaced shoulder-width apart so that the arms hang vertical and hands pass along the outer thighs.

Grip: An over–under grip with one palm facing forward and the other facing back prevents the bar from rolling.

Over–under grip

Stance: Position feet directly below the hips, with toes pointing straight ahead.

Trajectory: The bar should travel straight up and down, close to the body.

Range of motion: The barbell is lifted from the floor up to the top of the thighs, with arms extended and elbows kept stiff. During this movement, the erector spinae muscles work to stabilize and straighten the spine while the glutes and hamstrings generate hip extension. Keep the spine straight throughout the movement; do not round the lower back forward or extend the spine too far backward.

VARIATIONS

Stiff-leg deadlift: Performing the deadlift with the legs stiff shifts the focus from the lower back to the buttocks and hamstrings (see the stiff-leg deadlift on page 150).

Sumo-style deadlift: Performing the lift with a wide stance places the emphasis on the thigh muscles.

Cable pull-through: Stand facing away from a low pulley and perform the lift using a short bar with the cable passing between your legs.

Good Morning Lift

START

FINISH

Erector spinae group

Gluteus maximus

Hamstrings

Execution

1. Stand upright with a barbell resting across your shoulders.

2. Keeping your spine straight and knees stiff (straight or slightly bent), bend forward at the waist until your torso is just above parallel to the floor.

3. Raise your torso back to the upright position.

Muscles Involved

Primary: Erector spinae.

Secondary: Latissimus dorsi, gluteals, hamstrings.

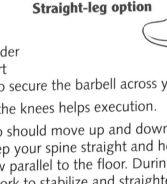

Straight-leg option

Anatomic Focus

Grip: Place hands slightly wider than shoulder-width apart using an overhand grip to secure the barbell across your shoulders.

Trajectory: A slight bend in the knees helps execution.

Range of motion: Your torso should move up and down through an arc of about 90 degrees. Keep your spine straight and head up, and avoid bending your torso below parallel to the floor. During this movement, the erector spinae muscles work to stabilize and straighten the spine while the glutes and hamstrings generate hip extension.

VARIATION

Machine Lift

You can perform this while seated with resistance provided by a pad across the upper back.

Your arm is divided into the upper arm and lower arm (forearm). The upper arm consists of one bone, the humerus, whereas the forearm consists of two bones, the radius (located on the thumb side) and ulna (on the little-finger side). The elbow is a hinge joint formed at the junction between the humerus, radius, and ulna. Two movements occur at the elbow joint: flexion and extension. During elbow flexion, the forearm moves toward the upper arm. During extension, the forearm moves away from the upper arm. Movement also takes place in the forearm when the radius rotates around the ulna. Supination (palm up) and pronation (palm down) take place between the radioulnar joints. The wrist joint is the junction between the lower end of the forearm bones and the small bones in the hand.

Biceps

As its name suggests, the biceps muscle has two heads. The short head attaches to the coracoid process, and the long head arises from above the glenoid of the shoulder joint. The two-headed muscle passes down alongside the humerus and attaches about 1.5 inches (4 cm) below the elbow joint onto a tuberosity on the inside of the radius bone. The biceps causes flexion at the elbow joint, raising the hand toward the face. The biceps also causes supination of the forearm, rotating the hand so the palm faces uppermost, the "get change" position.

In addition to the biceps, two other muscles flex (bend) the elbow: the brachialis and brachioradialis. The brachialis muscle lies deep beneath the biceps, arising from the lower half of the humerus and attaching to the ulna bone just below the elbow joint. So the brachialis lifts the ulna at the same time that the biceps lifts the radius. The brachioradialis muscle arises from the outer aspect of the lower end of the humerus and then travels down the forearm to attach to the radius just above the wrist joint.

Anatomy of the Biceps

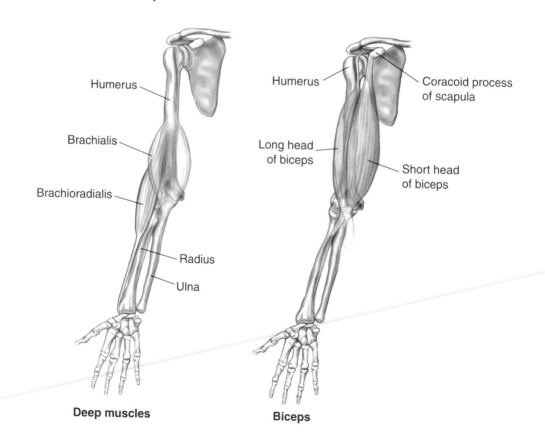

Humerus

Brachialis

Brachioradialis

Radius

Ulna

Deep muscles

Humerus

Coracoid process of scapula

Long head of biceps

Short head of biceps

Biceps

Triceps

The triceps muscle has three heads, or sections. The long head arises from beneath the glenoid fossa of the shoulder joint, the lateral (outer) head arises from the outer surface of the humerus, and the medial (inner) head from the medial and rear surfaces of the humerus. All three heads fuse at their lower ends to form a single tendon that attaches behind the elbow joint onto the olecranon process of the ulna bone. The triceps causes extension at the elbow, moving the hand away from the face. The triceps is the only muscle that straightens the elbow joint, whereas three muscles (biceps, brachialis, and brachioradialis) bend the elbow. All three heads of the triceps muscle cross the elbow joint, but the long head also crosses beneath the shoulder joint.

Anatomy of the Triceps

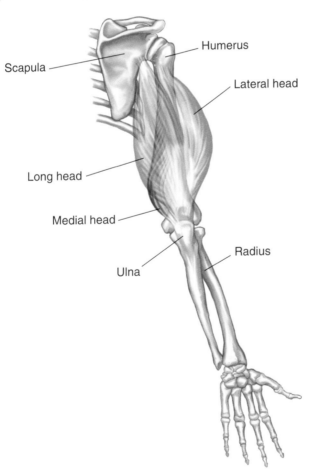

Scapula

Humerus

Lateral head

Long head

Medial head

Radius

Ulna

Forearm

The forearm is a mass of some 20 different muscles. It has two separate muscle compartments: the flexor group on the palm side and the extensor group on the reverse side. The fleshy muscle portions of almost all these muscles are located in the upper two-thirds of the forearm. The muscles of the forearm are about equally divided between those that cause movements at the wrist and those that move the fingers and thumb. Supination, rotating the hand so the palm faces up ("get change"), is performed by supinator and biceps muscles. Pronation, rotating the hand so the palm faces down ("give change"), is performed by the pronator teres and pronator quadratus.

Wrist flexors: Palmaris longus, flexor carpi radialis, flexor carpi ulnaris.

Finger flexors: Flexor digitorum superficialis, flexor digitorum profundus, flexor pollicis longus.

Wrist extensors: Extensor carpi radialis longus and brevis, extensor carpi ulnaris.

Finger extensors: Extensor digitorum, extensor pollicis longus and brevis, extensor indicis.

Hand supination: Supinator, biceps.

Hand pronation: Pronator teres, pronator quadratus.

Anatomy of the Forearm Flexors

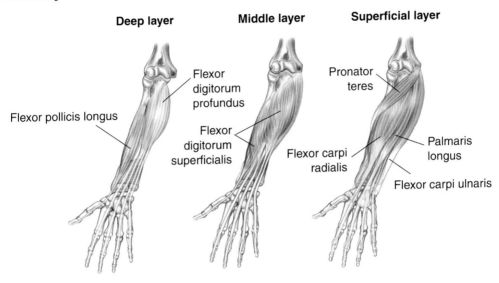

Deep layer

Middle layer

Superficial layer

Flexor pollicis longus

Flexor digitorum profundus

Flexor digitorum superficialis

Pronator teres

Flexor carpi radialis

Palmaris longus

Flexor carpi ulnaris

Anatomy of the Forearm Extensors

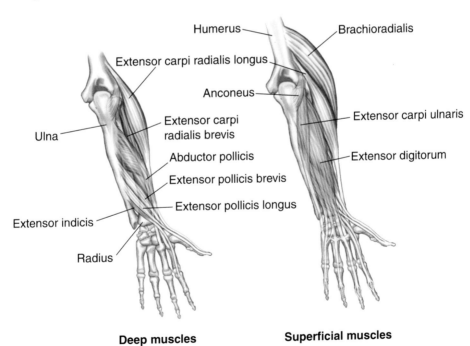

Humerus

Brachioradialis

Extensor carpi radialis longus

Anconeus

Extensor carpi ulnaris

Extensor carpi radialis brevis

Ulna

Abductor pollicis

Extensor digitorum

Extensor pollicis brevis

Extensor pollicis longus

Extensor indicis

Radius

Deep muscles

Superficial muscles

Barbell Curl

FINISH

Deltoid

Biceps:
Long head
Short head

START

Execution

1. Hold a barbell at arms' length, using a shoulder-width underhand grip.
2. Curl the bar up to shoulder level by bending your elbows.
3. Lower the bar back down to the arms' extended position.

Muscles Involved

Primary: Biceps.

Secondary: Brachialis, brachioradialis, anterior deltoid, forearm.

Anatomic Focus

Hand spacing: A wide grip focuses effort on the inner biceps (short head), whereas a narrow grip works the outer biceps (long head).

Wide grip

Narrow grip

Grip: With a straight bar, the underhand grip is fixed in supination (palms upward). Grip may be adjusted using an EZ bar (see Variation section).

Trajectory: The bar should move up and down in an arc close to the body. To isolate the biceps, motion should occur at the elbow and not the shoulder.

Range of motion: Stopping a few degrees short of full elbow extension keeps tension on the biceps as the barbell is lowered.

Body position: Stand upright with the spine straight. Tilting the torso is often used as a method of cheating the bar upward with momentum. Leaning slightly forward makes the initial phase of the curl easier. Leaning slightly backward helps complete the final phase of the repetition.

VARIATION

EZ Bar Curl

Performing the curl with an EZ bar changes the grip. The hands switch from the fully supinated (palms up) grip to a less supinated, nearly neutral grip (palms facing in). This hand position emphasizes the outer (long) head of the biceps and the brachialis, and it is less strenuous on the wrist joint.

Dumbbell Curl

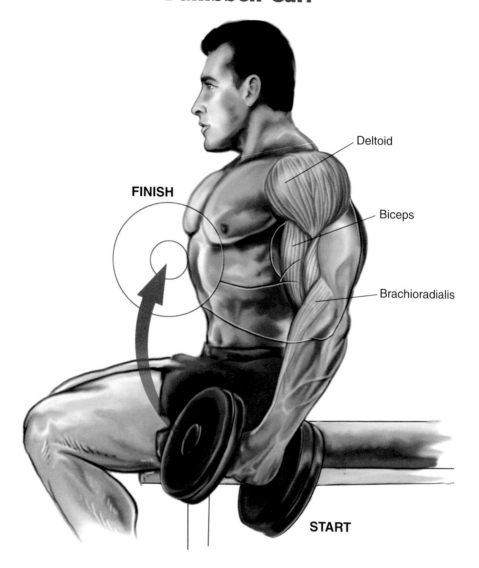

Deltoid

FINISH

Biceps

Brachioradialis

START

Execution

1. Hold a pair of dumbbells at arms' length by your sides, thumbs pointing forward.
2. One arm at a time, curl the dumbbell up toward your shoulder, rotating your hand so the palm faces upward.
3. Lower the dumbbell back down, and repeat with the opposite arm.

Muscles Involved

Primary: Biceps.

Secondary: Brachialis, brachioradialis, anterior deltoid, forearm.

Anatomic Focus

Grip: The dumbbell curl works the biceps in two ways: elbow flexion and forearm supination. Hence, to maximize biceps contraction, supinate the hand (palm uppermost) as the dumbbell is raised.

Finish position with hand supinated

Hand spacing: Instead of grasping the dumbbell in the middle of the bar, slide your palm over so your thumb rests against the inside of the plate. This grip change increases the load on the biceps during supination, activating more muscle fibers when the dumbbell is rotated.

Trajectory: Position your torso upright with the spine straight. Tilting the torso is often used as a method of cheating the weight upward with momentum. Leaning slightly forward makes the initial phase of the curl easier. Leaning slightly backward helps complete the final phase of the repetition.

Range of motion: Use a full range of motion at the elbow.

VARIATIONS

Standing dumbbell curl: This exercise can be performed in a standing position, but this requires muscular effort in the legs. The seated version of the exercise (illustrated) affords better focus.

Incline dumbbell curl: When performed while seated on an incline bench, effort is focused on the lower portion of the biceps, near the elbow.

Concentration Curl

Biceps

FINISH

START

Execution

1. Sit on the edge of a bench. Hold a dumbbell at arm's length, supporting your arm against the inside of your thigh.
2. Curl the dumbbell up toward your shoulder by bending at the elbow.
3. Lower the dumbbell back down to the start position.

Muscles Involved

Primary: Biceps.

Secondary: Brachialis, brachioradialis, forearm muscles.

Anatomic Focus

Grip: An underhand grip places the hand in supination and thereby maximizes biceps contraction.

Trajectory: The position of the upper arm (relative to the floor) changes the focus of effort. When the arm is vertical (shoulder directly above the elbow), resistance increases as the dumbbell is raised, and effort is focused on the upper biceps (peak). With the arm at an inclined angle (elbow in front of the shoulder), resistance is maximal at the start, so effort is targeted on the lower section of the biceps at the elbow.

Range of motion: Resting the upper arm against the thigh prevents movement at the shoulder and is an excellent way to isolate the biceps.

Vertical arm position, targeting upper biceps

Body position: The torso should remain motionless, supported by your free hand on the opposite thigh.

VARIATION

One-arm cable curl: You can also perform a concentration curl while using a D-handle attached to the cable of a low pulley (see the description for cable curl on page 104).

Cable Curl

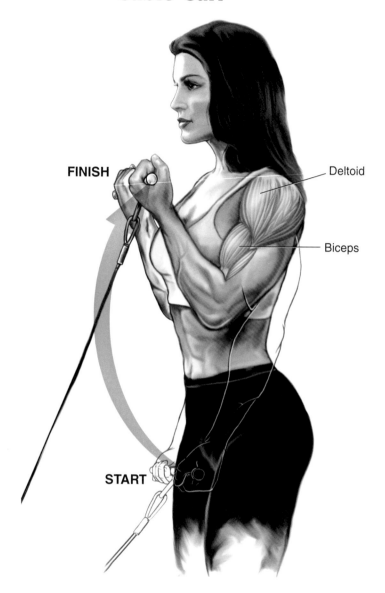

FINISH

START

Deltoid

Biceps

Execution

1. Grasp the short bar attached to a low pulley, using an underhand grip with arms straight.
2. Curl the bar up toward your shoulders by bending at the elbows.
3. Lower the weight down to the arms' extended position.

Muscles Involved

Primary: Biceps.

Secondary: Brachialis, brachioradialis, anterior deltoid, forearm.

Anatomic Focus

Hand spacing: A wider-than-shoulder-width grip focuses effort on the inner biceps (short head), whereas a narrow grip works the outer biceps (long head).

Grip: With a straight bar, the underhand grip is fixed in supination (palms upward). Using an EZ bar attachment, grip switches from the fully supinated position to a less supinated, nearly neutral grip (palms facing in). This hand position is less strenuous on the wrist joint and tends to emphasize the outer (long) head of the biceps and the brachialis muscle.

Body position: Stand upright with the spine straight.

Range of motion: Fixing the elbows against your sides prevents movement at the shoulder and is an excellent way to isolate the biceps.

Resistance: Unlike barbell or dumbbell curls where the resistance varies during the lift, the cable pulley provides a uniform resistance throughout the movement.

VARIATIONS

High-Pulley Curl

Grasp the D-handles attached to two high pulleys using an underhand grip, and stand midway between the pulleys. With your arms held at shoulder level, curl the handles toward your head. This version emphasizes the long head of the biceps and works the biceps peak.

One-Arm Cable Curl

Perform the exercise one arm at a time using a D-handle attached to the low pulley.

105

Preacher Curl

FINISH

Biceps

START

Execution

1. Sit with your upper arms resting on the preacher bench, and take a shoulder-width underhand grip on the bar with arms out straight.
2. Curl the bar up toward your shoulders.
3. Lower the weight back down to the arms' extended position.

Muscles Involved

Primary: Biceps.

Secondary: Brachialis, brachioradialis, forearm.

Anatomic Focus

Hand spacing: A wide grip focuses effort on the inner biceps (short head), whereas a narrow grip works the outer biceps (long head).

Grip: With a straight bar, the underhand grip is fixed in supination (palms upward). You may adjust the grip using an EZ bar (see Variations section).

Trajectory: With the upper arms supported at an inclined angle, resistance is maximal at the start, so effort is targeted on the lower section of the biceps near the elbow.

Range of motion: Resting the upper arms on the bench prevents movement at the shoulders and thereby helps isolate the biceps. Stopping a few degrees short of full elbow extension keeps tension on the biceps as the barbell is lowered.

Body position: Adjust the seat height so that your armpit is snug against the upper edge of the pad.

VARIATIONS

Dumbbell Preacher Curl

Performing the exercise one arm at a time with a dumbbell improves focus and isolation.

Dumbbell preacher curl

EZ Bar Preacher Curl

Using an EZ bar, the grip switches from the fully supinated (palms up) position to a less supinated, nearly neutral grip (palms facing in). This hand position tends to focus effort on the outer (long) head of the biceps and the brachialis muscle, and it is less strenuous on the wrist joint.

EZ bar preacher curl

Machine Curl

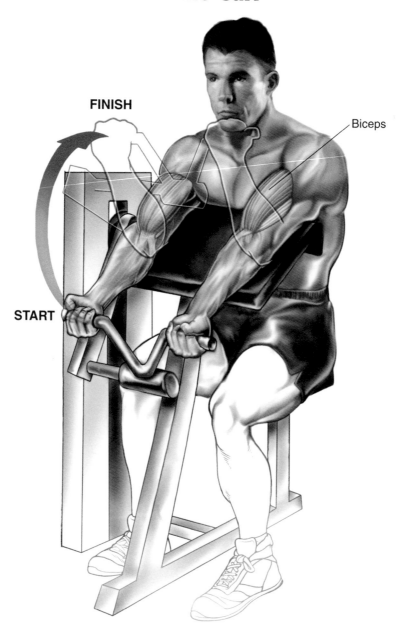

FINISH

Biceps

START

Execution

1. Grasp the bar using a shoulder-width underhand grip, with your elbows resting on the pad and arms out straight.
2. Curl the bar toward your shoulders by bending at the elbow.
3. Return the bar to the arms' extended position.

Muscles Involved

Primary: Biceps.

Secondary: Brachialis, brachioradialis, forearm.

Anatomic Focus

Hand spacing: A wide grip focuses effort on the inner biceps (short head), whereas a narrow grip works the outer biceps (long head).

Grip: An angled handlebar is less strenuous on the wrist joint.

Trajectory: Depending on the design of the machine, an incline arm pad focuses effort on the lower portion of the biceps, whereas a flat horizontal pad emphasizes the middle-biceps peak.

Range of motion: Effort focuses on the lower biceps during the initial phase of the curl, then switches to the middle biceps (peak) as the weight is raised.

Resistance: Unlike barbell or dumbbell curls, where the resistance varies during the lift, the machine provides a uniform resistance throughout the movement.

VARIATIONS

Flat-Pad Machine Curl

In contrast to an incline arm pad, the trajectory of a flat horizontal arm pad focuses on the biceps peak.

Additional variation:

One-arm machine curl: Performing the exercise one arm at a time improves focus and isolation.

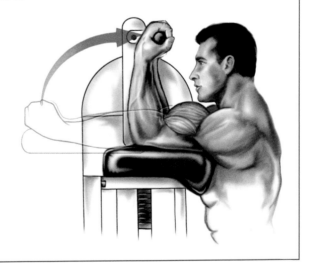

Triceps Pushdown

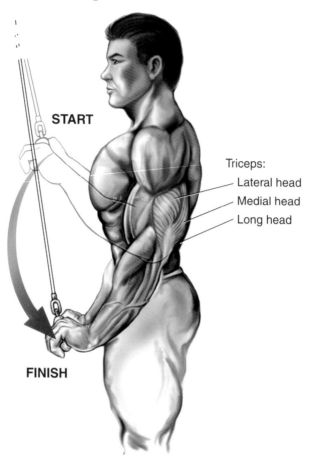

START

Triceps:
Lateral head
Medial head
Long head

FINISH

Execution

1. Take a shoulder-width overhand grip on a short bar attached to the high pulley.
2. Begin with the bar at chest level, elbows bent a little more than 90 degrees.
3. Keeping your upper arms stiff, push the bar down until your elbows lock out.

Muscles Involved

Primary: Triceps.

Secondary: Deltoid, forearm.

Anatomic Focus

Hand spacing: A wide grip focuses effort on the inner triceps (long head), whereas a narrow grip focuses on the outer triceps (lateral head).

Grip: Using the straight bar, a pronated grip (palms down) emphasizes the outer lateral head of the triceps, whereas a supinated grip (palms up) focuses effort on the inner long head. An angled V-shaped bar switches the hands into a neutral grip (thumbs up) that targets all three heads of the triceps equally.

Trajectory: With the upper arms perpendicular to the floor, the outer triceps (lateral head) contributes to the movement. If you perform the exercise with your arms raised parallel to the floor, you focus effort on the inner triceps (long head).

Range of motion: Fixing the upper arms against your sides prevents movement at the shoulder and is an excellent way to isolate the triceps. Motion should occur through the elbow only.

Resistance: Unlike barbell or dumbbell exercises, where the resistance varies during the lift, the cable provides a uniform resistance throughout the movement.

Body position: Standing upright with the spine straight is the standard position. Leaning the torso slightly forward at the waist provides better stability when using heavier weights.

VARIATIONS

Rope Pushdown

The rope attachment affords a forcible pronation at the wrist, which targets the outer lateral head of the triceps.

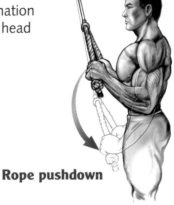

Rope pushdown

Reverse-grip pushdown

Reverse-Grip Pushdown

A reverse underhand grip focuses effort on the inner long head of the triceps.

Additional variation:

One-arm pushdown: Performing the exercise one arm at a time with the D-handle, using an overhand or underhand grip, focuses effort and improves isolation.

Dip

FINISH

Triceps:
Long head
Medial head
Lateral head

Anterior deltoid

START

Pectoralis major

Execution

1. Grasp the parallel bars and lift yourself up until your arms are fully extended.
2. Bend your elbows and slowly lower your body until your upper arms are approximately parallel to the floor; keep your torso upright.
3. Push yourself back up, straightening your arms until the elbows lock out.

Muscles Involved

Primary: Triceps.

Secondary: Chest, anterior deltoid, forearm.

Anatomic Focus

Hand spacing: When the apparatus allows, a wide grip focuses effort on the inner triceps (long head), whereas a narrow grip focuses on the outer triceps (lateral head).

Grip: The standard grip, palms facing together with thumbs forward, hits all three heads of the triceps, with an emphasis on the inner long head. Reversing the grip so that the palms face outward with thumbs facing back switches most of the effort to the outer triceps (long head).

Trajectory: Keeping the elbows close to your sides helps isolate the triceps. Flaring the elbows out wide allows the chest muscles to assist.

Range of motion: To isolate the triceps, movement should occur primarily at the elbow, so keep motion at the shoulder to a minimum.

Body position: To focus effort on the triceps, keep your body upright. Leaning forward makes the chest muscles do more work.

Resistance: Resistance is provided by your body weight and is not easily adjusted. You can add resistance by attaching a weighted belt around your hips.

Reverse grip

VARIATION

Machine Dip

Performing the exercise while seated in the triceps pushdown (dip) machine, where the resistance is adjustable, makes it easier to focus your effort on the triceps. All the tips mentioned previously for the parallel-bar dip also apply to the machine variation.

Lying Triceps Extension

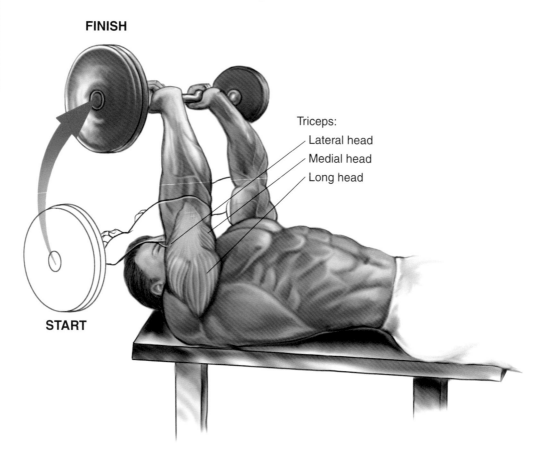

FINISH

START

Triceps:
Lateral head
Medial head
Long head

Execution

1. Lying on a flat bench, hold a barbell at arms' length above your chest with a narrow overhand grip, hands approximately 6 inches (15 cm) apart.
2. Bend at the elbows and lower the bar down to touch your forehead.
3. Push the bar upward until your elbows lock out.

Muscles Involved

Primary: Triceps.

Secondary: Chest, deltoid, forearm.

Anatomic Focus

Hand spacing: A wide grip emphasizes the inner triceps (long head), whereas a narrow grip targets the outer triceps (lateral head). Keep the elbows close, and do not allow them to flare outward to the sides.

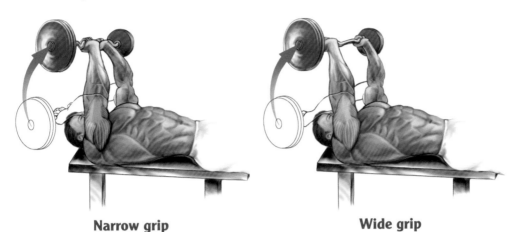

Narrow grip   **Wide grip**

Grip: Using a straight bar, you may perform this exercise with an overhand (pronated) grip or an underhand (supinated) grip. Using an EZ bar or dumbbells (see Variations section) requires a neutral grip. An overhand grip works the inner (long) head, an underhand grip emphasizes the outer (lateral) head, and a neutral grip works all three heads of the triceps.

Trajectory: The vertical position of the arm stretches the inner (long) head of the triceps, so this exercise targets this section of the muscle. Lowering the bar beyond the forehead toward the bench generates a greater stretch in the long head, favoring its contraction during the movement.

Body position: Keep your elbows pointing up and upper arms vertical. Do not lower the bar toward your face or chin, because this causes the elbows to drop and allows the deltoid and pectoral muscles to assist in the movement.

Range of motion: To isolate the triceps, motion should occur only at the elbow, not at the shoulder.

VARIATIONS

Dumbbell lying triceps extension: Perform the exercise with a dumbbell in each hand; thumbs should point toward your face (neutral grip).

Reverse grip: You can also perform the exercise while using a reverse (supinated) grip on the bar to emphasize the outer (lateral) head of the triceps.

Seated Triceps Press

FINISH

Triceps:
Medial head
Long head

START

Execution

1. Sit upright while holding a barbell in both hands at arms' length above your head; use a narrow overhand grip.
2. Bend at the elbows and lower the bar down behind your head.
3. Push the bar upward until your elbows lock out.

Muscles Involved

Primary: Triceps.

Secondary: Deltoid, forearm.

Anatomic Focus

Hand spacing: A wide grip emphasizes the inner triceps (long head), whereas a narrow grip targets the outer triceps (lateral head). Keep the elbows close together, and do not allow them to flare outward.

Grip: Using a straight bar, this exercise requires an overhand (pronated) grip. Using an EZ bar or a dumbbell (see the Variations section) requires a neutral grip. An overhand grip works the inner (long) head, whereas a neutral grip works all three heads of the triceps.

Trajectory: The vertical position of the arm stretches the inner long head of the triceps, so this exercise preferentially targets this section of the muscle.

Range of motion: To isolate the triceps, motion should occur at the elbow only.

Safety: The triceps extension exercise poses two safety concerns. First, it places excessive stretch on the triceps tendon; second, it places the shoulder joint in a vulnerable position for injury. Therefore, it is not the best exercise choice for people who have elbow or shoulder pain.

VARIATIONS

Single-Dumbbell Seated Triceps Press

You may perform this exercise one arm at a time while holding a dumbbell with the palm facing forward to emphasize the outer (lateral) head of the triceps.

Additional variation:

EZ bar triceps press: Performing this movement with an EZ bar offers a variety of grip choices.

Close-Grip Bench Press

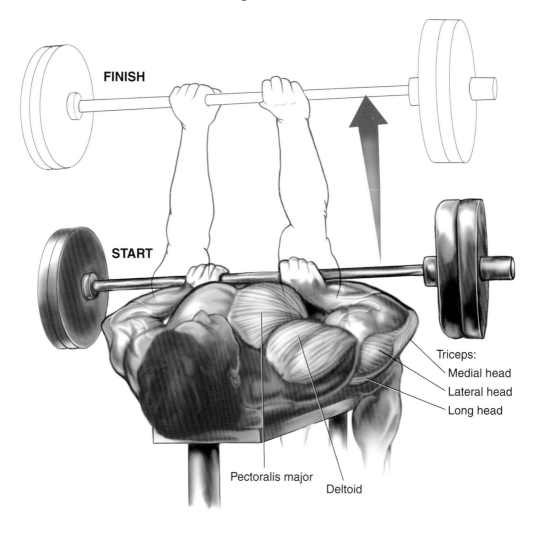

FINISH

START

Triceps:
Medial head
Lateral head
Long head

Pectoralis major

Deltoid

Execution

1. Take a narrow (6-inch, or 15-centimeter) overhand grip on the bar.
2. Lower the weight down slowly to touch the middle chest.
3. Push the bar straight up until your elbows lock out.

Muscles Involved

Primary: Triceps, pectoralis major.
Secondary: Anterior deltoid.

Anatomic Focus

Hand spacing: To target the triceps, hand spacing should be narrower than shoulder width.

Grip: An underhand (supinated) grip on the bar also targets the triceps, but this grip requires the hands to be spaced wide apart (see Variation section).

Trajectory: Keep your elbows close to your sides to emphasize the triceps, not the chest.

Range of motion: A full range of motion (achieving full lockout) is required for maximizing triceps effort.

VARIATION

Reverse Grip Bench Press

Performing the bench press using an underhand grip (palms facing up) with hands spaced more than shoulder-width apart also targets the triceps.

Dumbbell Kickback

Lateral head of triceps

Medial and long heads
of triceps

FINISH

START

Execution

1. Grab a dumbbell in one hand, bend forward at the waist, and support your torso by resting your free hand on a bench or on your knee.
2. Begin with your upper arm parallel to the floor and elbow bent at 90 degrees.
3. Raise the dumbbell upward, straightening your arm until the elbow locks out.

Muscles Involved

Primary: Triceps.

Secondary: Rear deltoid, latissimus dorsi.

Anatomic Focus

Grip: A neutral grip (thumb forward) works all sections of the triceps. Rotating the dumbbell so your palm faces up targets the outer (lateral) head.

Trajectory: Keep the upper arm parallel to the floor and the elbow close to your side.

Range of motion: To isolate the triceps, movement should occur at the elbow, and the shoulder should remain stiff.

Resistance: Because of the effect of gravity, resistance is variable and increases as the dumbbell is raised upward.

Body position: Your torso should be slightly above parallel to the floor. If you stand too upright, you can't perform the exercise effectively.

VARIATION

Cable Kickback

You can perform this exercise while using a D-handle attached to a low pulley. Unlike the dumbbell version, where the resistance varies during the lift, the cable provides a uniform resistance throughout the movement.

Wrist Curl

Pronator teres
Flexor carpi ulnaris
Palmaris longus
Flexor carpi radialis
Flexor digitorum superficialis
Flexor pollicis longus

FINISH

START

Execution

1. While seated on the edge of a bench, grasp a barbell with a shoulder-width underhand grip, and rest the back of your forearms on your thighs.
2. Lower the bar by bending your wrists down toward the floor.
3. Curl the weight up by using wrist motion.

Muscles Involved

Primary: Forearm flexors.

Secondary: Finger flexors.

Anatomic Focus

Hand spacing: The ideal hand spacing is shoulder width or slightly narrower. Your hands should be directly in line with your forearms to minimize unnecessary stress in the wrist joint.

Grip: This exercise requires an underhand (supinated) grip with the palms facing upward. Your thumbs may grip under or over the bar, depending on personal preference. One advantage of a "thumbless" grip is that it allows you to lower the bar farther, increasing the range of motion (see the next section).

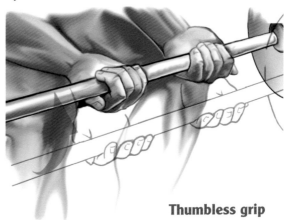

Thumbless grip

Range of motion: Letting the bar roll down your fingers during the lowering phase of the repetition increases the range of motion. As the bar is curled upward, the finger flexors work as you finger-curl the bar into your palm, and then the forearm flexors work as you curl the wrist upward. Because the finger flexors make up a significant portion of the forearm muscles, this extended repetition is more effective for building forearm mass.

Trajectory: Changing the position of your forearms in relation to the floor alters the resistance and adjusts the focus of the exercise. When your forearms are flat and parallel to the floor, resistance is maximal at the beginning and decreases as the bar is lifted upward. When your forearms make an angle with the floor, such that your elbows are higher than your wrists, resistance is minimal at the start and increases as the bar is curled up. This second variation is more effective at maximizing forearm contraction.

Body position: Your forearms may be supported in different positions:

1. Between your legs on a flat bench
2. On top of your thighs while seated on a bench
3. On the incline pad of a preacher bench

VARIATIONS

Dumbbell wrist curl: You can also perform this exercise one arm at a time while using a dumbbell.

Preacher bench wrist curl: Perform the exercise with your forearms resting on the incline pad of a preacher bench.

Reverse Wrist Curl

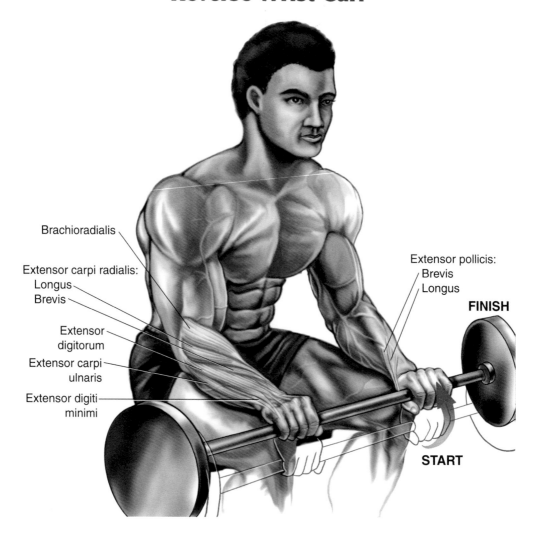

Brachioradialis

Extensor carpi radialis:
Longus
Brevis

Extensor
digitorum

Extensor carpi
ulnaris

Extensor digiti
minimi

Extensor pollicis:
Brevis
Longus

FINISH

START

Execution

1. Grasp a barbell using an overhand grip, and rest your forearms on top of your thighs or on the edge of a bench.
2. Lower the bar by bending your wrists toward the floor.
3. Raise the weight up using wrist motion.

Muscles Involved

Primary: Forearm extensors.

Secondary: Finger extensors and flexors.

Anatomic Focus

Hand spacing: The ideal hand spacing is shoulder width or narrower. Your hands should be directly in line with your forearms.

Grip: This exercise requires an overhand (pronated) grip with the palms facing down and your thumbs gripped around the bar.

Trajectory: Changing the position of your forearms in relation to the floor alters the resistance and adjusts the focus of the exercise. When your forearms are flat and parallel to the floor, resistance is maximal at the beginning and decreases as the bar is lifted upward. When your forearms make an angle with the floor such that your elbows are higher than your wrists, resistance is minimal at the start and increases as the bar is curled up. This second variation is more effective at maximizing forearm contraction.

Range of motion: Use a full range of motion to maximize forearm effort.

Body position: Your forearms may be supported in different positions:

1. Between your legs on a flat bench
2. On top of your thighs while seated on a bench
3. On the incline pad of a preacher bench
4. Held parallel to the floor (unsupported) in the standing curl position

---

VARIATIONS

Dumbbell Reverse Wrist Curl

You can also perform this exercise one arm at a time while using a dumbbell.

Additional variation:

Preacher bench: Perform the exercise with your forearms resting on the incline pad of a preacher bench.

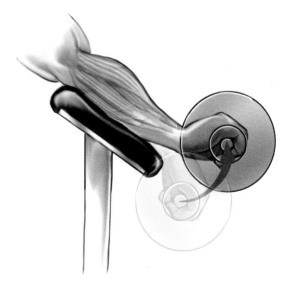

Reverse Barbell Curl

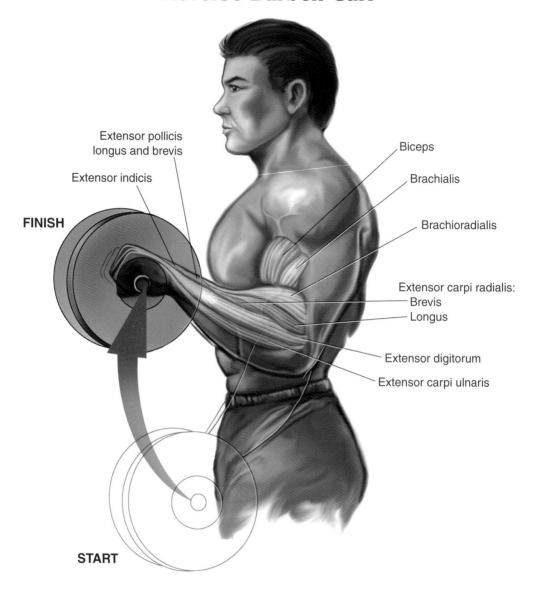

Extensor pollicis
longus and brevis

Extensor indicis

FINISH

Biceps

Brachialis

Brachioradialis

Extensor carpi radialis:
Brevis
Longus

Extensor digitorum

Extensor carpi ulnaris

START

Execution

1. Hold a barbell at arms' length using a shoulder-width overhand grip.
2. Raise the bar up toward shoulder level, curling your wrists up and back as you bend the elbows.
3. Lower the bar back down to the arms' extended position, dropping the wrists.

Muscles Involved

Primary: Forearm extensors, finger extensors.

Secondary: Biceps, brachioradialis, brachialis.

Anatomic Focus

Grip: This exercise requires an overhand (pronated) grip with the palms facing down and your thumbs gripped around the bar.

Hand spacing: The ideal hand spacing is shoulder width with your hands directly in line with your forearms.

Range of motion: To maximize forearm involvement, be sure to achieve a full range of motion at the wrist. Cock the wrist back into full extension as the bar is raised, and flex the wrist down as the weight is lowered.

Resistance: Because of gravity, resistance increases as the bar is raised upward. To ensure maximum forearm effort, delay the wrist extension curl until the forearms are parallel to the floor.

Full wrist extension

VARIATIONS

Reverse dumbbell curl: You can also perform this exercise while using dumbbells with an overhand, pronated grip.

Wrist roller: Attach a small weight plate to the center of a short broomstick using a strong rope. Holding the broomstick out in front of you, wrist-curl the rope around the stick, thereby raising the weight upward.

Hammer Curl

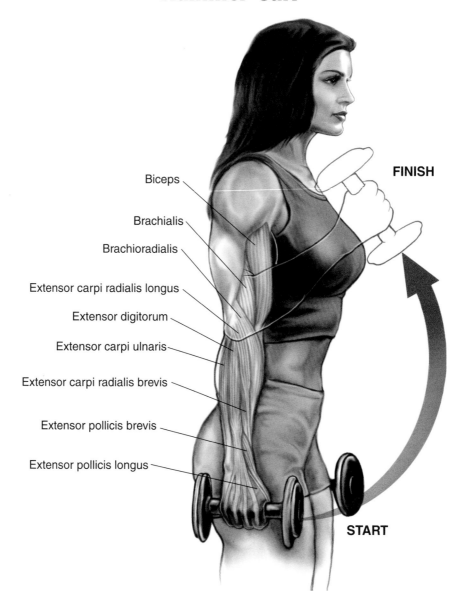

Biceps

Brachialis

Brachioradialis

Extensor carpi radialis longus

Extensor digitorum

Extensor carpi ulnaris

Extensor carpi radialis brevis

Extensor pollicis brevis

Extensor pollicis longus

FINISH

START

Execution

1. Hold a dumbbell in each hand with your palms facing inward (thumbs pointing forward).
2. Curl one dumbbell at a time up toward your shoulder, keeping your palms facing inward.
3. Lower the dumbbell back down to the arm's extended position, and repeat with the opposite arm.

Muscles Involved

Primary: Brachioradialis.

Secondary: Brachialis, forearm extensors and flexors, biceps.

Anatomic Focus

Grip: This exercise requires a neutral grip with the palms facing inward, thumbs wrapped around the dumbbell bar.

Range of motion: To maximize forearm effort, work your wrist in the vertical plane, cocking your thumb upward as the dumbbell is raised.

Trajectory: To focus effort on the brachioradialis, raise the dumbbell across the front of your body rather than at your side.

Raising the dumbbell across the body to focus on brachioradialis

The leg is divided into the upper leg (thigh) and lower leg (calf). The upper leg consists of one bone, the femur, whereas the lower leg consists of two bones, the tibia (located on the big-toe side) and fibula (on the little-toe side). The knee is a hinge joint formed at the junction between the femur and the tibia. Two movements occur at the knee joint: flexion and extension. During knee flexion, the lower leg bends toward the back of the thigh. During knee extension, the lower leg moves away from the thigh so the leg becomes straight. The hip is a ball-and-socket joint between the upper end of the femur and the pelvic bone. Six main movements occur at the hip joint: flexion, extension, abduction, adduction, internal rotation, and external rotation. During hip flexion, the thigh bends up toward the abdomen, whereas during hip extension, the thigh moves backward toward the buttocks. The thighs separate apart during hip abduction, and the thighs come together during hip adduction. The ankle is a hinge-type joint between the lower tibia and fibula and the talus bone in the foot. During ankle dorsiflexion, the toes lift off the floor and the foot moves toward the shin. During ankle plantar flexion, the heel lifts off the floor and the foot moves away from the shin.

Quadriceps

The quadriceps femoris, located in front of the thigh, has four separate heads:

1. Rectus femoris arises from the front of the pelvic bone.
2. Vastus medialis arises from the inner edge of the femur.
3. Vastus lateralis arises from the outer edge of the femur.
4. Vastus intermedius arises from the front surface of the femur and lies underneath the rectus femoris.

The four heads merge together, attach onto the patella (knee cap), and then insert via a single (patellar) tendon onto the tibia, just below the knee joint. The main function of the quadriceps is to extend the knee and straighten the leg. Because the rectus femoris arises from the pelvic bone, contraction of this muscle also flexes the hip joint.

Anatomy of the Legs, Front View

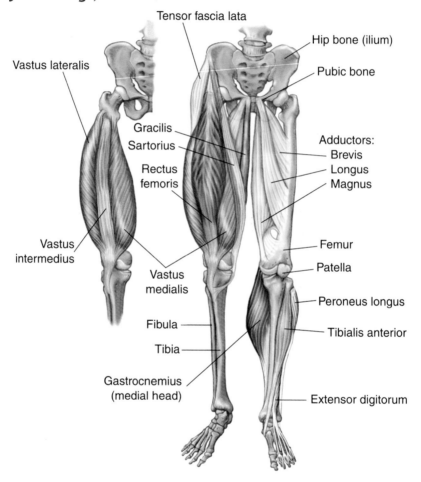

Tensor fascia lata

Hip bone (ilium)

Pubic bone

Vastus lateralis

Gracilis

Sartorius

Adductors:
Brevis
Longus
Magnus

Rectus
femoris

Vastus
intermedius

Femur

Patella

Vastus
medialis

Peroneus longus

Fibula

Tibialis anterior

Tibia

Gastrocnemius
(medial head)

Extensor digitorum

Hamstrings

The hamstrings, located behind the thigh, are a group of three muscles that originate from the ischium bone of the pelvis.

1. Biceps femoris passes behind the outer aspect of the thigh to attach to the head of the fibula bone, just below the knee.
2. Semimembranosus passes behind the inner aspect of the thigh, attaching to the upper tibia bone behind the knee.
3. Semitendinosus passes behind the inner aspect of the thigh, attaching to the upper tibia bone adjacent to semimembranosus.

All three hamstrings span both the knee and hip joints. Therefore, they serve dual functions: flexion of the knee and extension of the hip.

Gluteals

The gluteus maximus arises from a large area on the rear of the pelvic bone, passes down behind the hip joint, and attaches to the upper femur. This powerful muscle causes hip extension. Good exercises for building the gluteal muscles are the squat, deadlift, and lunge.

Other thigh muscles include the following:

Hip adductors (inner thigh): Gracilis; adductor longus, magnus, and brevis

Hip abductors: Tensor fascia latae; gluteus medius and minimus

Hip flexors: Sartorius, iliopsoas, rectus femoris

Anatomy of the Legs and Glutes, Rear View

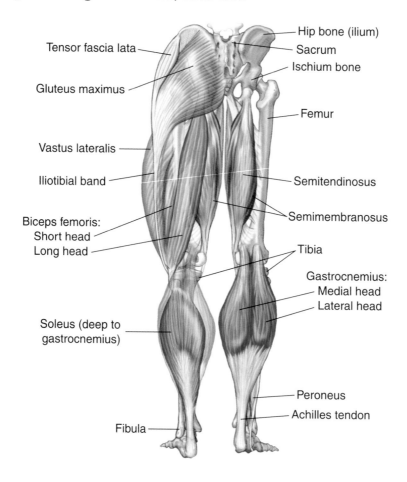

Tensor fascia lata

Gluteus maximus

Vastus lateralis

Iliotibial band

Biceps femoris:
Short head
Long head

Soleus (deep to
gastrocnemius)

Fibula

Hip bone (ilium)

Sacrum

Ischium bone

Femur

Semitendinosus

Semimembranosus

Tibia

Gastrocnemius:
Medial head
Lateral head

Peroneus

Achilles tendon

Calves

The lower leg contains 10 different muscles. The calf comprises two muscles:

1. Gastrocnemius is the visible muscle of the calf. The two heads (medial and lateral) of the gastrocnemius arise from the rear of the femur bone, immediately above the knee joint.
2. Soleus arises from the rear aspect of the tibia and lies underneath the gastrocnemius.

The tendons of the gastrocnemius and soleus fuse to form the Achilles tendon that passes behind the ankle joint and attaches to the calcaneus (heel bone). The calf muscles cause plantar flexion of the ankle, the movement required for standing on tiptoes. The relative contribution of the two calf muscles depends on the angle of knee flexion. The gastrocnemius is the prime mover when the leg is straight, and the soleus becomes more active as the knee bends. Note that the gastrocnemius crosses both the knee and ankle joints, and therefore serves a double function: knee flexion and ankle flexion.

The following are other lower-leg muscles:

Ankle extension (dorsiflexion): Tibialis anterior

Ankle eversion: Peroneus longus and brevis

Ankle inversion: Tibialis posterior

Toe flexors and extensors: Flexor digitorum longus, flexor hallucis longus, extensor digitorum longus, and extensor hallucis longus

Leg Extension

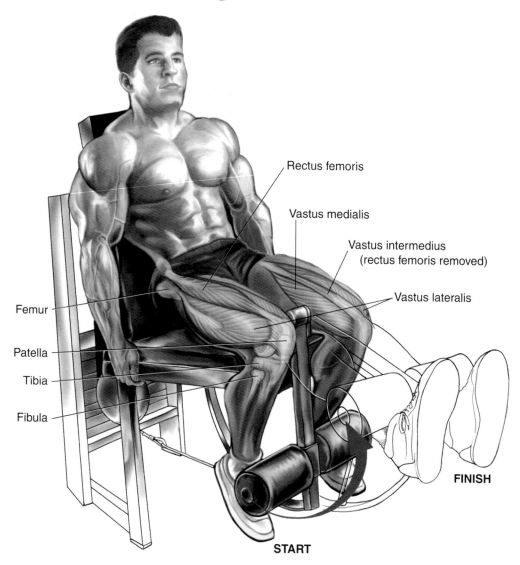

Rectus femoris

Vastus medialis

Vastus intermedius
(rectus femoris removed)

Vastus lateralis

Femur

Patella

Tibia

Fibula

START

FINISH

Execution

1. Sit on machine and place ankles under the roller pads.
2. Raise legs upward until knees are straight.
3. Lower legs back down to start position, knees bent 90 degrees.

Muscles Involved

Primary: Quadriceps.
Secondary: Tibialis anterior.

Anatomic Focus

Foot position: Pointing your toes directly upward *(a)* hits all sections of the quadriceps equally. Pointing your toes inward *(b)* internally rotates the tibia to target the inner quad "teardrop" (vastus medialis). Pointing your toes outward *(c)* externally rotates the tibia to hit the outer quad (vastus lateralis).

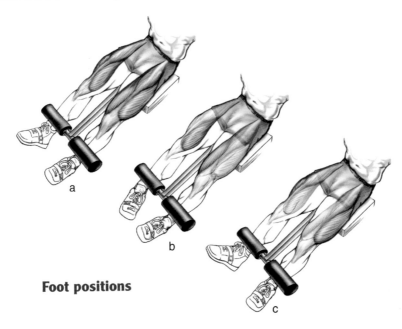

Foot positions

Foot spacing: There isn't much space on the roller pads to adjust foot spacing, but placing your feet close together will tend to target the outer quad, and a wider spacing will focus a little more on the inner quad.

Body position: Adjust the backrest so that the back of your knee fits snugly against the front edge of the seat and your whole thigh is supported. Leaning your torso backward or raising your buttocks off the seat extends the hip joint stretching the rectus femoris, making this section of the quad work harder during the exercise.

Range of motion: The arc of motion should be approximately 90 degrees. Forcibly contract the quadriceps at the top when the knees are fully straight. To avoid excess stress on the patella (kneecap), do not bend the knees beyond 90 degrees.

Resistance: Resistance is fairly uniform, but on many new machines the resistance increases slightly as the weight is raised up. Less resistance at the start position minimizes stress across the kneecap with the knee bent.

VARIATION

One-leg extension: Performing this exercise one leg at a time improves focus. The unilateral leg extension is particularly useful for improving thigh asymmetry or aiding in rehabilitation when one leg is injured.

Barbell Squat

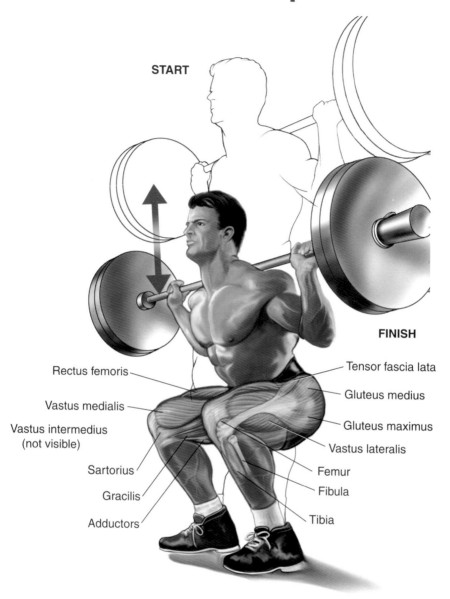

START

FINISH

Rectus femoris

Vastus medialis

Vastus intermedius (not visible)

Sartorius

Gracilis

Adductors

Tensor fascia lata

Gluteus medius

Gluteus maximus

Vastus lateralis

Femur

Fibula

Tibia

Execution

1. Stand with a barbell across your shoulders, feet shoulder-width apart.
2. Slowly bend your knees until your thighs are parallel with the floor.
3. Straighten your legs to return to the start (upright) position.

Muscles Involved

Primary: Quadriceps, gluteals.

Secondary: Hamstrings, adductors, spinal erectors, abdominals.

Anatomic Focus

Stance widths

Foot spacing: A narrow stance (a) shifts focus to the outer quads (vastus lateralis) and abductors (tensor fascia latae). A shoulder-width stance (b) targets the whole thigh. A wider stance (c) places more emphasis on the inner quads, adductor muscles, and sartorius.

Foot position: Your toes should point in the same direction as your thigh and knee: forward or slightly outward.

Positioning: Placing a 1-inch (2.5 cm) block under both heels shifts the weight forward, placing more emphasis on the quads and less on the gluteals. This adjustment is also useful for those with less flexible ankles and hips. Positioning the bar lower on the trapezius and shoulders improves balance while shifting focus to the gluteals; it is a technique used by powerlifters to lift more weight.

Body position: Keep your spine straight and head up at all times. Ensure your hands are placed equidistant from the center of the bar, and maintain a firm grip throughout the movement. Inhale deeply during the downward phase and exhale on the way up. Do not bend your torso forward, because this can cause back injury.

Range of motion: As the weight is lowered, stop when your knees bend to a 90-degree angle and your thighs are parallel to the floor. Squatting below parallel increases the risk of knee and spine injury.

VARIATIONS

Front squat: Performing the squat with the barbell held across the front of your shoulders shifts the emphasis to the quads, away from the gluteals. The front squat poses a higher degree of difficulty and requires lighter weights.

Machine squat: Performing this exercise using a machine, such as a Smith machine, helps balance and improves safety.

QUADRICEPS

Leg Press

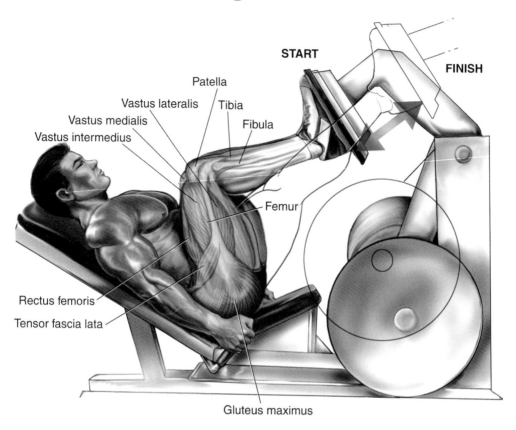

Patella

Vastus lateralis

Tibia

Vastus medialis

Fibula

Vastus intermedius

START

FINISH

Femur

Rectus femoris

Tensor fascia lata

Gluteus maximus

Execution

1. Sit in the leg press machine and place your feet shoulder-width apart on the footplate.
2. Slowly lower the weight until your knees bend to 90 degrees.
3. Push the weight back to the beginning position by straightening your legs.

Muscles Involved

Primary: Quadriceps.

Secondary: Gluteals, hamstrings, adductors.

Anatomic Focus

Foot position: Placing your feet low on the footplate *(a)* emphasizes the quadriceps. Positioning your feet higher on the footplate *(b)* switches the focus to the gluteals and hamstrings.

Foot spacing: Placing your feet shoulder-width apart targets the whole thigh. A wider foot spacing *(a)* places more emphasis on the inner quads (vastus medialis), adductor muscles, and sartorius. Placing your feet close together *(b)* shifts focus to the outer quads (vastus lateralis) and abductors (tensor fascia latae).

Trajectory: Pushing the weight up using the balls of your feet and allowing your heels to rise off the footplate as the weight is lowered will target the quads and reduce load across your kneecap. Pushing the weight through the heels of your feet targets the hamstrings and gluteals.

Body position: The angle your torso makes with your legs influences muscular focus and the amount of stress through your lower back. When the angle between the seat and back rest is 90 degrees, emphasis is placed on the gluteals and hamstrings, but this acute angle places more stress on your lower back. If the backrest is tilted lower toward the floor, your torso leans back; this places less stress across your lower spine and places more emphasis on the quads.

Range of motion: Stopping a few degrees short of full lockout at the top keeps tension on the quads.

Resistance: In comparison with the barbell squat, the seated leg press reduces the axial load on your spine and reduces the risk of backache. Furthermore, the leg press emphasizes the quadriceps, not the gluteals.

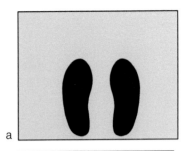

a

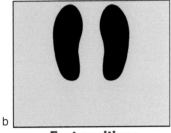

b

Foot positions

a

b

Foot spacing

VARIATION

One-leg press: Performing this exercise one leg at a time is useful in focusing effort on a lagging thigh or protecting a leg when it is injured.

Hack Squat

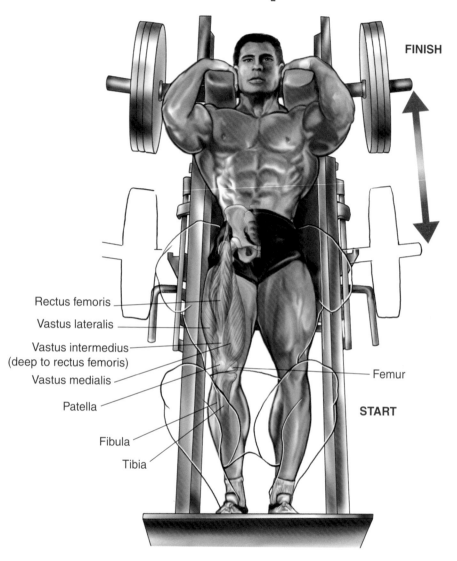

FINISH

Rectus femoris

Vastus lateralis

Vastus intermedius
(deep to rectus femoris)

Vastus medialis

Patella

Fibula

Tibia

Femur

START

Execution

1. Place your back against the backrest and shoulders under the pads, and stand with your feet shoulder-width apart on the footplate, toes pointing forward.
2. Slowly lower the weight, bending your knees to 90 degrees.
3. Push the weight back to the beginning position by straightening your legs.

Muscles Involved

Primary: Quadriceps.

Secondary: Gluteals, hamstrings, adductors.

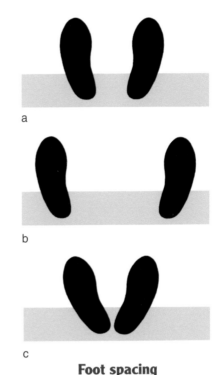

Anatomic Focus

Foot spacing: Placing your feet shoulder-width apart *(a)* targets the whole thigh. A wider foot spacing *(b)* places more emphasis on the inner quads, adductor muscles, and sartorius. Placing your feet close together *(c)* shifts focus to the outer quads (vastus lateralis) and abductors (tensor fascia latae).

Foot position: Your toes should point in the same direction as your thigh and knee: forward or slightly outward. Placing your feet low on the footplate (close to your body) emphasizes the quadriceps, whereas placing your feet higher on the footplate requires more effort from the gluteals and hamstrings.

Trajectory: Pushing the weight using the forefoot and allowing your heels to rise off the footplate as the weight is lowered helps isolate the quads and reduces stress across the kneecaps.

Foot spacing

Body position: Keep your spine flat against the backrest.

Range of motion: Stopping a few degrees short of full lockout at the top keeps tension on the quads.

Resistance: In comparison with the barbell squat, the hack squat backrest provides support to your spine. Furthermore, the hack squat places more emphasis on the quadriceps and less on the gluteals.

VARIATIONS

Dumbbell squat: Squatting while holding dumbbells at arms' length at your sides is a variation that combines elements of the barbell squat and the hack squat, but your grip is the weakest link.

Reverse hack squat: Performing the hack squat while facing the machine switches the focus to the gluteals and hamstrings.

Lunge

START

FINISH

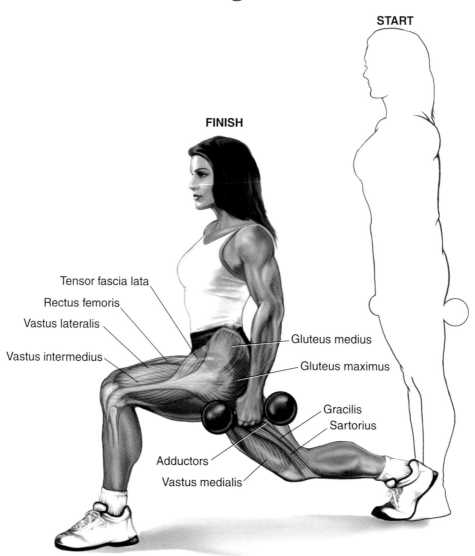

Tensor fascia lata

Rectus femoris

Vastus lateralis

Vastus intermedius

Gluteus medius

Gluteus maximus

Gracilis
Sartorius

Adductors

Vastus medialis

Execution

1. Stand with feet shoulder-width apart while holding two dumbbells at arms' length by your sides.
2. Step forward and bend the knee until your leading thigh is parallel with the floor.
3. Return to the start position and repeat, using the opposite leg.

Muscles Involved

Primary: Quadriceps, gluteals.

Secondary: Hamstrings, adductors.

Anatomic Focus

Foot spacing: A stable, shoulder-width stance works best to maintain balance.

Foot position: Point your toes straight ahead or slightly outward as you step forward. The back foot stays fixed to the floor in the same spot.

Trajectory: Take a shorter step (lunge) to target the quadriceps. A larger step places the emphasis on the gluteals and hamstrings.

Body position: As you lunge forward, place your body weight on the leading leg. Keep your torso upright and your back straight.

Range of motion: During the lunge, your knee should bend 90 degrees, with your thigh parallel to the floor.

Resistance: The lunge requires a lighter weight than most other leg exercises. Using a weight that is too heavy may cause pain in the kneecaps.

VARIATIONS

Barbell Lunge

Instead of holding two dumbbells at arms' length by your sides, rest a barbell across your shoulders. Compared to barbell lunges, dumbbell lunges make it easier to maintain balance.

Additional variations:

Walking lunge: Instead of returning to the same start position, do a lunge walk. Perform lunges, one leg after another, so that you walk the length of the gym floor (or a parking lot or field).

Smith machine lunge: This is similar to the barbell lunge, but the machine provides stability and balance.

Lying Leg Curl

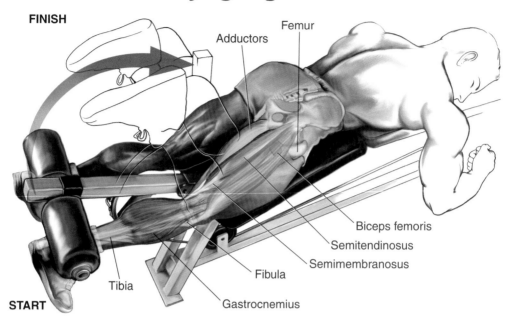

FINISH

START

Femur
Adductors
Biceps femoris
Semitendinosus
Semimembranosus
Fibula
Gastrocnemius
Tibia

Execution

1. Lie facedown on the machine and hook your heels under the roller pads.
2. Curl the weight by bending your knees, and raise your heels toward your buttocks.
3. Lower the weight back down to the start position.

Muscles Involved

Primary: Hamstrings.

Secondary: Gluteals, calf muscles.

Anatomic Focus

Foot position: Pointing your toes straight *(a)* targets all three hamstring muscles. Pointing the toes inward *(b)* emphasizes the inner hamstrings (semimembranosus and semitendinosus), whereas pointing the toes outward *(c)* focuses effort on the outer hamstrings (biceps femoris). Keeping your ankles bent at 90 degrees (dorsiflexed) minimizes contribution from the calf muscles and thereby helps isolate the hamstrings. Pointing your feet (tiptoe position) allows the calf muscles to participate in the exercise.

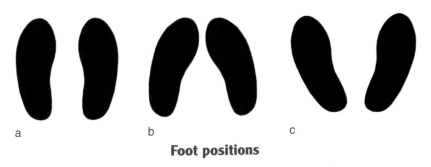

a   b   c

Foot positions

Foot spacing: Placing your feet hip-width apart is the standard position. Wide foot spacing targets the inner hamstrings (semimembranosus and semitendinosus), whereas narrow foot spacing emphasizes effort of the outer hamstrings (biceps femoris). Foot spacing is limited by the size of the roller pad.

Body position: The padded surface of most machines is angled at hip level, bending your torso forward slightly. This body position tilts your pelvis and stretches the hamstrings, thereby helping isolate the muscles. Keep your spine straight, and do not raise your chest upward.

Range of motion: Bend your knees as far as possible during the upward phase. Stop a few degrees short of full extension at the bottom to keep tension on the hamstrings and minimize stress across the knee joint.

Resistance: Resistance is fairly uniform, but on many new machines the resistance is lower at the start position, where the hamstrings are fully stretched and most vulnerable to injury.

VARIATION

Seated leg curl: The upright backrest of the seated leg curl machine creates a 90-degree hip flexion angle between your torso and thighs. While this body position affords a greater stretch, it prevents the hip extension that is required for a maximum contraction in the hamstrings.

Standing Leg Curl

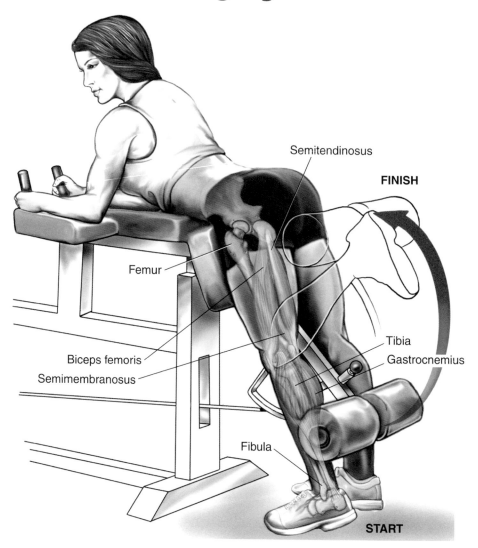

Semitendinosus

FINISH

Femur

Biceps femoris

Semimembranosus

Tibia

Gastrocnemius

Fibula

START

Execution

1. Hook one heel under the roller pad, and support your weight with the other leg.
2. Curl the weight by bending your knee, raising your heel toward your buttock.
3. Lower the weight back down to the start position.

Muscles Involved

Primary: Hamstrings.

Secondary: Gluteals, calf muscles.

Anatomic Focus

Foot position: Pointing your toes straight down *(a)* targets all three hamstring muscles. Pointing the toes inward *(b)* tends to emphasize the inner hamstrings (semimembranosus and semitendinosus), whereas pointing the toes outward *(c)* focuses effort on the outer hamstrings (biceps femoris). Keeping your ankles bent at 90 degrees (dorsiflexed) minimizes contribution from the calf muscles and thereby helps isolate the hamstrings.

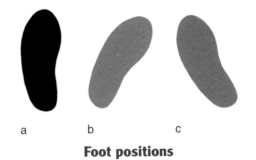

a   b   c

Foot positions

Body position: The padded surface of most machines is angled at hip level, bending your torso forward slightly. This body position tilts your pelvis and stretches the hamstrings, thereby helping to isolate the muscles. Depending on the machine design, your supporting leg may take a standing or kneeling position (see the Variation section).

Range of motion: Bend your knees as full as possible during the upward phase. Stop a few degrees short of full extension at the bottom to keep tension on the hamstrings and minimize stress across the knee joint.

Resistance: In contrast to the lying leg curl, the standing leg curl is performed one leg at a time, which helps muscle isolation and focus. Resistance is fairly uniform, but on many new machines the resistance is lower at the start position when the hamstrings are fully stretched and most vulnerable to injury.

VARIATION

Kneeling leg curl: Using this machine, your nonworking leg is supported by kneeling on a pad, and your torso is supported on your elbows. Because your torso is bent forward at the waist, the hamstrings are stretched—an advantage over the exercise on the standing leg curl machine.

Stiff-Leg Deadlift

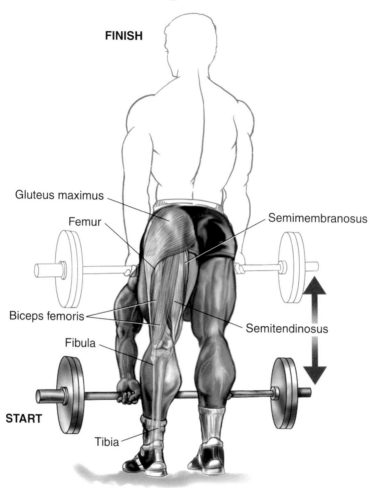

FINISH

Gluteus maximus

Femur

Semimembranosus

Biceps femoris

Semitendinosus

Fibula

START

Tibia

Execution

1. Stand upright with feet directly below your hips, holding a barbell at arms' length.
2. Bend forward at the waist, lowering the weight down but keeping your legs stiff.
3. Stop before the weight touches the floor, and raise it back up.

Muscles Involved

Primary: Hamstrings, gluteals.

Secondary: Spinal erectors, quadriceps.

Anatomic Focus

Foot spacing: Position feet directly below the hips. A wide stance places more emphasis on the inner hamstrings.

Foot position: Point toes directly forward or slightly out.

Grip: Hands should be spaced shoulder-width apart so that the arms hang vertical and hands pass along the outer thighs. An over–under grip with one palm facing forward and the other facing back prevents the bar from rolling.

Trajectory: The bar should travel straight up and down, close to the body.

Body position: Knees may be slightly bent but should be kept stiff in order to isolate the hamstrings. Keep your back straight throughout the movement. Performing this exercise with the balls of both feet on a half-inch-thick (1.3 cm) weight plate is a safe way to prestretch the hamstrings.

Range of motion: Lower the weight until your hamstrings reach full stretch without rounding your spine. There is no need to perform this exercise while standing on a bench or block as a means of increasing the range of motion. When your pelvis achieves full forward tilt, the hamstrings are at full stretch. Bending your lower spine does not have any effect on the hamstrings or increase the range of downward motion. Rounding your lower spine merely increases the risk of injury. Depending on your flexibility, the barbell should be lowered to a point below your knees or just above the ankles.

Resistance: The stiff-leg deadlift for hamstrings requires a lighter weight than that used during the traditional powerlift for strengthening the lower back (see page 88).

VARIATION

Dumbbell Stiff-Leg Deadlift

You can also perform this exercise while holding a dumbbell in each hand at arms' length.

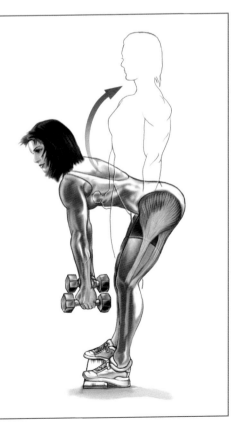

Standing Calf Raise

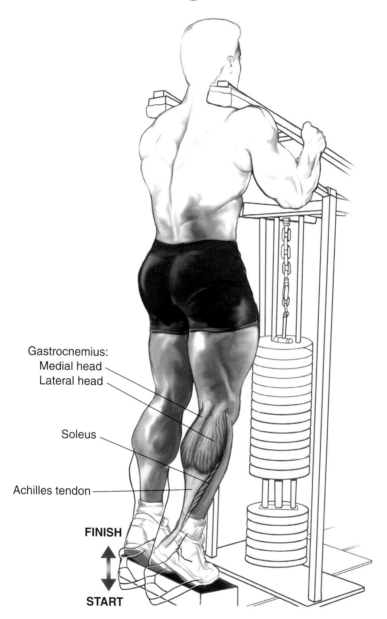

Gastrocnemius:
Medial head
Lateral head

Soleus

Achilles tendon

FINISH

START

Execution

1. Stand with your toes on the platform and shoulders under the pads, and lower your heels as far as possible for a full stretch.
2. Lift the weight by raising your heels as high as possible, keeping your legs straight.
3. Slowly lower your heels back down to the start position.

Muscles Involved

Primary: Gastrocnemius.

Secondary: Soleus.

Anatomic Focus

Foot position: Pointing your toes straight ahead *(a)* targets the whole gastrocnemius muscle. Pointing your toes outward *(b)* emphasizes the inner (medial) head, whereas pointing your toes inward *(c)* targets the outer (lateral) head.

Foot spacing: Positioning your feet hip-width apart targets the whole gastrocnemius muscle. A wide stance *(a)* tends to emphasize the inner (medial) head, whereas a narrow stance *(b)* targets the outer (lateral) head.

Body position: Keep your knees stiff and back straight. Keeping your knees locked straight stretches the gastrocnemius, which helps to focus effort on the gastrocnemius and minimizes soleus action. If your knees bend, the soleus is allowed to contribute to the movement.

Range of motion: To maximize the range of motion, aim for a full stretch at the bottom and full squeeze at the top.

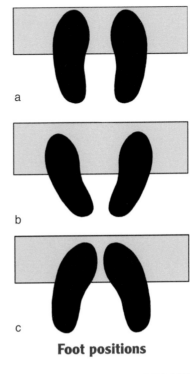

a

b

c

Foot positions

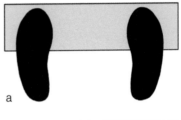

a

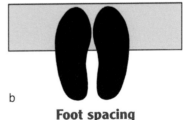

b

Foot spacing

VARIATIONS

Smith machine raise: You can perform this exercise at the Smith machine while standing on a thick block of wood.

One-leg calf raise: Perform calf raises one leg at a time, holding a dumbbell in your hand on the same side.

Donkey Calf Raise

Gastrocnemius:
Medial head
Lateral head

Soleus

Achilles tendon

FINISH

START

Execution

1. Place your toes on a block, lean forward while supporting your torso on the bench, and lower your heels as far as possible.
2. Lift the weight by raising your heels up as high as you can, keeping your legs straight.
3. Slowly lower your heels down to the start position.

Muscles Involved

Primary: Gastrocnemius.

Secondary: Soleus.

Anatomic Focus

Foot position: Pointing your toes straight ahead *(a)* targets the whole gastrocnemius muscle. Pointing your toes out *(b)* emphasizes the inner (medial) head, whereas pointing your toes inward *(c)* targets the outer (lateral) head.

Foot spacing: Positioning your feet hip-width apart targets the whole gastrocnemius muscle. A wide stance emphasizes the inner (medial) head, whereas a narrow stance targets the outer (lateral) head.

Body position: Keep your spine straight and torso parallel to the floor. Keeping your knees fully straight helps isolate the gastrocnemius. A slight bend at the knees allows the soleus to contribute to the movement.

Range of motion: To maximize the range of motion, aim for a full stretch at the bottom and full squeeze at the top.

Resistance: Have a training partner straddle your hips, as shown in the illustration, so that his or her body weight provides resistance.

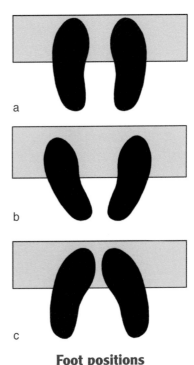

Foot positions

VARIATION

Machine donkey calf raise: You can perform this exercise while using a machine where the weight is transmitted through a pad resting across your lower back.

Machine Calf Raise

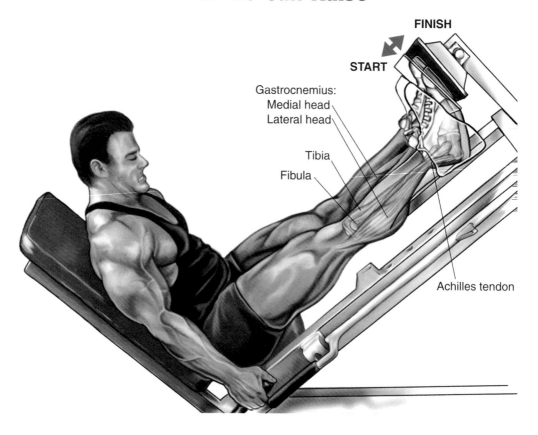

Execution

1. Place the balls of your feet on the edge of the footplate (such as on a leg press machine), and lower the weight as far as possible.
2. Push the weight up as far as you can, contracting your calf muscles.
3. Slowly lower the weight down to the start position.

Muscles Involved

Primary: Gastrocnemius.

Secondary: Soleus.

Anatomic Focus

Foot position: Point your toes straight ahead *(a)* to target the whole gastrocnemius muscle. Point your toes out *(b)* to emphasize the inner (medial) head, or point your toes inward *(c)* to target the outer (lateral) head of the gastrocnemius.

Foot spacing: Positioning your feet hip-width apart targets the whole gastrocnemius muscle. A wide stance emphasizes the inner (medial) head, whereas a narrow stance targets the outer (lateral) head.

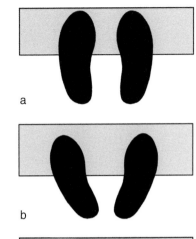

a

b

Body position: In biomechanical terms, this exercise could be called a seated straight-leg calf raise. Keep your knees stiff so that movement occurs exclusively at the ankle. Keeping your knees fully straight helps isolate the gastrocnemius. A slight bend at the knees allows the soleus to contribute to the movement.

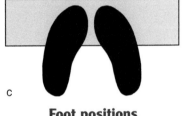

c

Foot positions

Range of motion: To maximize the range of motion, aim for a full stretch at the bottom and full squeeze at the top.

Resistance: On the leg press machine, resistance is transmitted through the footplate. Since the knees are held straight and the torso is bent at 90 degrees to your legs, this exercise is similar to the donkey calf raise described earlier.

VARIATION

Calf-sled machine: This is another way to perform seated straight-leg calf raises.

Seated Calf Raise

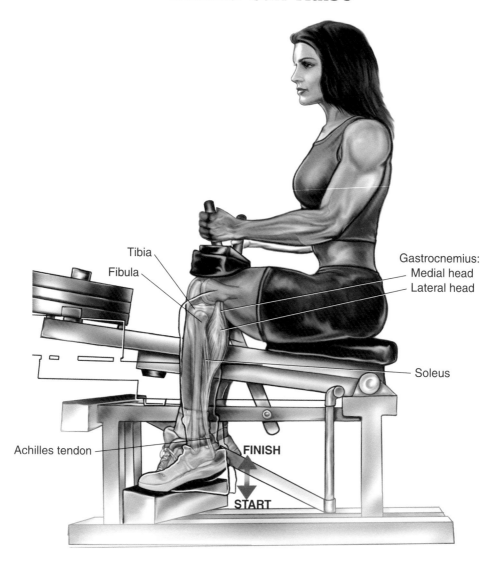

Tibia
Fibula
Gastrocnemius:
Medial head
Lateral head
Soleus
Achilles tendon
FINISH
START

Execution

1. Place the balls of your feet on the platform, place the pads across your lower thighs, and lower your heels as far as possible.
2. Lift the weight by raising your heels up as high as you can.
3. Slowly lower your heels down to the start position.

Muscles Involved

Primary: Soleus.

Secondary: Gastrocnemius.

Anatomic Focus

Foot position: Pointing your toes straight ahead *(a)* targets the whole calf muscle. Pointing your toes out *(b)* emphasizes the inner calf, whereas pointing your toes inward *(c)* targets the outer section of the muscle.

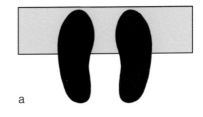

a

Foot spacing: Positioning your feet hip-width apart targets the whole calf muscle. A wide stance emphasizes the inner (medial) head, whereas a narrow stance targets the outer (lateral) head.

b

Body position: Position the pad just above your knees, not too high on the thighs. In the seated position, the bent knee places emphasis on both the soleus and the gastrocnemius.

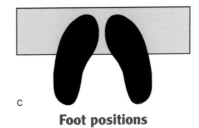

Range of motion: To maximize the range of motion, aim for a full stretch at the bottom and full squeeze at the top.

c

Foot positions

VARIATION

Seated barbell calf raise: Perform the exercise while seated on a bench. Toes are on a block and a barbell rests across your lower thighs.

The abdominal wall can be divided into two separate anatomic parts, each of which functions differently.

The front wall consists of one muscle, the rectus abdominis (also known as the "abs"). This muscle arises from the lower margin of the rib cage and sternum and passes vertically downward to attach on the pubic bone. The two rectus abdominis muscles (one on each side) are encased in a sheath of fascia that forms the central demarcation down the middle of the abs, known as the linea alba. Fascia divisions in the muscles are responsible for the "six-pack" appearance. The rectus muscles cause flexion of the trunk, bending the torso forward toward the legs. The motion is carried out by the upper abs, which pull the rib cage down toward the pelvis, or by the lower abs, which lift the pelvis upward toward the chest.

The side wall consists of three layers of muscles. The external oblique is the outer visible layer that passes obliquely downward from the rib cage to the pelvic bone. The middle layer is the internal oblique that passes obliquely upward from the pelvic bone to the ribs. Internal oblique lies under external oblique, and the fibers of the two muscles pass at right angles to one another. The innermost layer is the transversus abdominis, which lies horizontally across the abdominal wall. Contraction of the oblique muscles on one side causes the torso to bend sideways. Contraction of the obliques simultaneously on both sides assists the rectus muscle in flexing the trunk and also splints the abdominal wall whenever a weight is lifted. Note that only the outer external oblique is visible.

The serratus anterior muscle forms part of the side wall of the chest. This muscle arises from the scapula behind and passes forward around the chest wall to attach to the upper eight ribs. The serrated edge of this muscle emerges from beneath the outer margin of the pectoralis muscle, sending fingerlike projections into the external oblique. The serratus anterior pulls (or protracts) the scapula forward, stabilizing the scapula against the chest wall. The serratus anterior provides an essential accessory function whenever the pectoralis major and latissimus dorsi muscles contract. It can also be targeted during exercises that work the oblique muscles.

An effective abdominal workout should include exercises that target all areas of your midsection. For your upper abs select a crunch or sit-up. For your lower abs choose from leg raises, knee-ups, or reverse crunches. To complete your workout, target the side wall with a twisting maneuver, oblique crunch, or side bend.

Anatomy of the Abdominal Wall

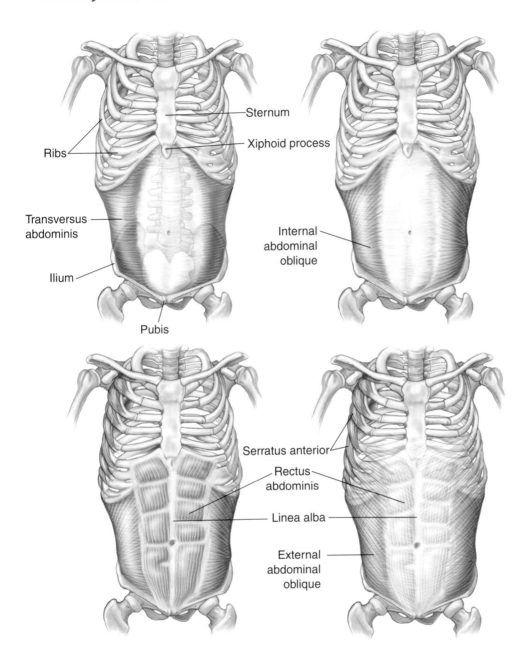

Sternum

Xiphoid process

Ribs

Transversus abdominis

Internal abdominal oblique

Ilium

Pubis

Serratus anterior

Rectus abdominis

Linea alba

External abdominal oblique

Sit-Up

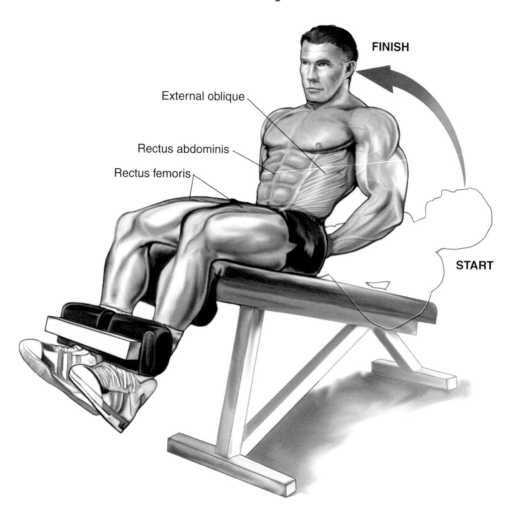

FINISH

External oblique

Rectus abdominis

Rectus femoris

START

Execution

1. Hook your feet under the pad and sit on the decline bench with your torso upright.
2. Lower your torso backward until it is almost parallel to the floor.
3. Return to the upright position by bending at the waist.

Muscles Involved

Primary: Rectus abdominis.

Secondary: Quadriceps, hip flexors.

Anatomic Focus

Hand position: You may hold your hands together behind your lower back, cross them in front of your chest, or interlock them behind your head. As your hands shift position from your lower back to your chest to your head, the relative resistance increases.

Foot position: Secure your feet under a roller pad or comparable support.

Body position: Bend your knees to reduce stress on the lower back.

Range of motion: Your torso should be vertically upright in the sitting position, with your abdomen almost touching the thighs. Lower your torso backward until it is almost parallel to the floor, about three-quarters of the way down. Do not lean back too far, because when tension is released from the abdominals, stress is placed on the lower back.

Trajectory: Tilting the bench at a steeper angle makes the exercise more difficult.

Resistance: Add resistance by tilting the bench at a steeper angle or holding a weight plate on your chest.

VARIATIONS

Floor Sit-Up

You can perform this exercise while seated on the floor with your knees bent and your feet secured on the floor.

Additional variation:

Twisting sit-up: See description of this exercise on page 180.

Crunch

FINISH

START

Rectus femoris

Rectus abdominis

Serratus anterior   External oblique

Execution

1. Lie flat on the floor, hips bent at 90 degrees, with hands behind your head.
2. Raise your shoulders off the floor, crunching your chest forward, keeping your lower back in contact with the floor.
3. Lower your shoulders back to the start position.

Muscles Involved

Primary: Rectus abdominis (upper).

Secondary: Obliques.

Anatomic Focus

Hand position: You may position your hands at your sides or across your chest, or you may interlock them behind your head. As your hands shift position from your sides to your chest to your head, the resistance increases.

Foot position: You may place your feet on the floor close to your buttocks or elevate them on a bench. Resistance is increased with your legs elevated.

Body position: Your thighs should be bent at an angle of 90 degrees to your torso. Your lower legs may be supported on top of a flat bench, or your feet can be positioned on the floor close to your buttocks.

Legs supported

Range of motion: The crunch motion occurs in the upper spine, and your shoulders rise a few inches off the floor. Your lower back remains in contact with the floor, and there is no motion at the hips. This is in contrast to the sit-up, where the movement occurs at the waist and hips.

Resistance: You can increase the degree of difficulty by placing your hands behind your head or by elevating your legs on a bench.

VARIATIONS

Reverse crunch: See description of this exercise on page 178.

Oblique crunch: See description of this exercise on page 182.

Rope Crunch

START

Serratus anterior

External oblique

FINISH

Rectus abdominis

Execution

1. Kneel on the floor beneath a high pulley, and grab the rope attachment with both hands behind your head.
2. Crunch the weight downward, curling your torso and bending at the waist.
3. Return to the start position.

Muscles Involved

Primary: Rectus abdominis.

Secondary: Obliques, serratus anterior.

Anatomic Focus

Hand position: Your hands may hold the rope above your head, on either side of your head, or in front of your upper chest. The higher your hands are held, the greater the difficulty.

Body position: You may perform this exercise while facing toward or away from the weight stack, depending on personal preference.

Range of motion: Your torso should move from the upright position to almost parallel with the floor.

Trajectory: If you position yourself a short distance away from the pulley, you will benefit from a greater range of motion when you crunch.

Resistance: Alter resistance by adjusting the weight stack.

Facing pulley

VARIATION

Machine rope crunch: A variety of machines replicate the rope crunch, where your back is supported while you sit or stand to perform the exercise.

Machine Crunch

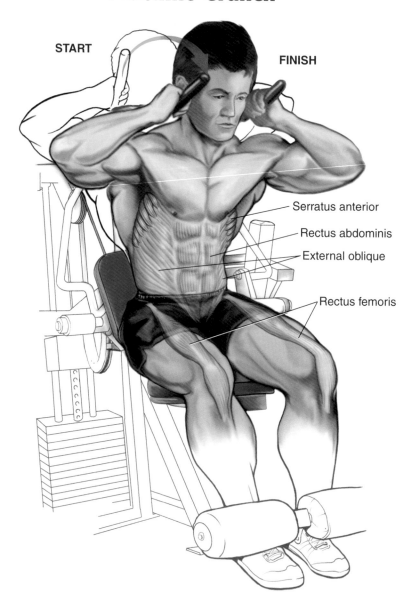

START

FINISH

Serratus anterior

Rectus abdominis

External oblique

Rectus femoris

Execution

1. Sit in the seat, grasp the handles, and place your feet under the ankle pads.
2. Crunch down, curling your torso toward your knees.
3. Return to the upright position.

Muscles Involved

Primary: Rectus abdominis.

Secondary: Obliques, serratus anterior.

Anatomic Focus

Hand position: Depending on the machine's design, your hands grasp handles alongside your head, or your hands simply rest on the chest pad.

Foot position: Feet may be positioned on the floor or hooked under ankle pads, depending on the machine's design.

Body position: On some machines the handles provide resistance, while on other machines resistance is transmitted via a chest pad.

Range of motion: Your torso should move from the upright position to almost parallel with the floor.

Resistance: Depending on the machine's design, you move the weight by holding on to handles or moving a chest pad. Adjust the weight stack to vary the resistance.

VARIATION

Machine Crunch With Chest Pad

On some abdominal machines, the resistance is provided by way of a chest pad.

Incline Leg Raise

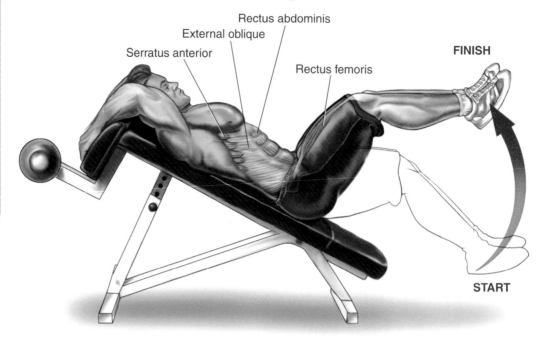

Serratus anterior
External oblique
Rectus abdominis
Rectus femoris
FINISH
START

Execution

1. Lie supine on an inclined abdominal bench with your legs down.
2. Raise your legs at the hips and pull your thighs toward your chest, keeping your knees slightly bent.
3. Slowly lower your legs back down to the start position.

Muscles Involved

Primary: Rectus abdominis (lower).

Secondary: Obliques, hip flexors (iliopsoas, rectus femoris).

Anatomic Focus

Hand position: Your hands function to stabilize your torso by grasping the bench or handles above your head.

Foot position: Keep your feet together, knees slightly bent.

Body position: Your upper torso should remain in contact with the bench. As you raise your legs up, lift your pelvis off the bench slightly to maximize contraction in the lower abdominals.

Range of motion: To maximize muscle contraction on the way up, raise your knees as high as possible toward your chest. To keep tension on the abs, do not lower your legs all the way down or allow your feet to touch the floor.

Trajectory: The angle that the bench makes with the floor affects the degree of difficulty. Titling the bench at a steeper angle makes the exercise harder.

Resistance: Decrease the incline by lowering the bench to reduce resistance, or increase the incline by raising the bench to increase resistance.

VARIATION

Incline Leg Raise With Weight

This exercise can be performed holding a dumbbell between your feet for added resistance.

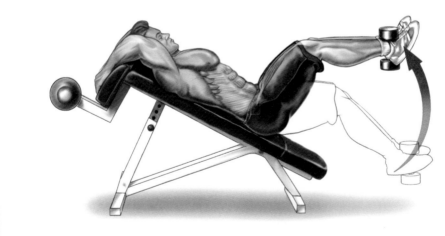

Hanging Leg Raise

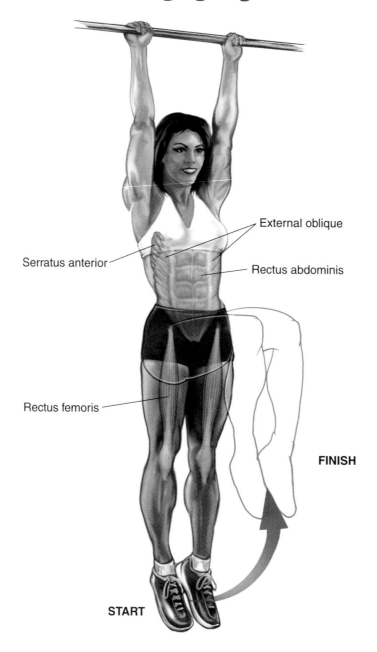

External oblique

Serratus anterior

Rectus abdominis

Rectus femoris

FINISH

START

Execution

1. Hang from a chin-up bar using your hands, or place your elbows in a pair of ab slings (these attach to the bar to support your body weight); your legs hang down.
2. Lift both knees, together and slightly bent, toward your chest.
3. Slowly lower your legs back down to the start position without swinging.

Muscles Involved

Primary: Rectus abdominis.

Secondary: Obliques, hip flexors (iliopsoas, rectus femoris).

Anatomic Focus

Hand position: Take a shoulder-width overhand grip on the chin-up bar and hang with your arms straight. Alternatively, use a pair of supportive upper-arm sleeves, like the ab sling device.

Foot position: Keep your feet together, knees slightly bent.

Body position: Your torso should hang vertical, perpendicular to the floor.

Range of motion: Raise your knees as high as possible to maximize muscular effort. As you lower your legs down, keep your knees slightly bent to maintain tension on the abs.

Trajectory: As you raise your legs up, lift your pelvis to maximize contraction in the lower abdominals.

Resistance: The exercise is harder if you try to keep your legs straight. The more you bend your knees, the easier the exercise becomes.

VARIATION

Vertical Leg Raise

On this apparatus, your back is supported against a backrest and your elbows rest on pads. This version prevents the legs and torso from swinging.

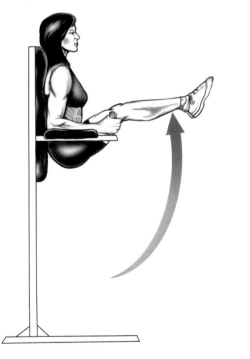

Knee-Up

Psoas major

Iliacus

Rectus abdominis

External oblique

Rectus femoris

FINISH

START

Execution

1. Sit on the edge of a flat bench, legs hanging down with knees slightly bent, and grip the bench behind you.
2. Raise your knees up toward your chest, keeping your legs together.
3. Lower your legs back down until your heels almost touch the floor.

Muscles Involved

Primary: Rectus abdominis.

Secondary: Obliques, hip flexors (iliopsoas, rectus femoris).

Anatomic Focus

Hand position: Grasp the bench behind your hips for support.

Foot position: Keep your feet together and knees slightly bent.

Body position: Lean back slightly so that your torso makes a 45- to 60-degree angle with the bench.

Range of motion: Raise your knees up until your thighs almost touch your abdomen. As you lower your legs down, stop before your heels make contact with the floor to keep tension on the muscles.

Trajectory: Leaning your torso back allows you to increase the range of motion.

Resistance: Hold a small dumbbell between your ankles to add resistance.

Side view

Reverse Crunch

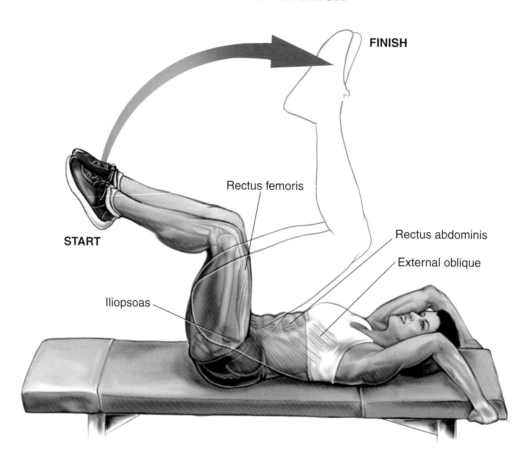

FINISH

START

Rectus femoris

Rectus abdominis

External oblique

Iliopsoas

Execution

1. Lie on a flat bench, position your feet so you have a 90-degree bend at your knees and hips, and grasp the bench behind your head for support.
2. Lift your pelvis off the bench until your feet point to the ceiling.
3. Lower your legs back to the start position.

Muscles Involved

Primary: Rectus abdominis.

Secondary: Obliques, hip flexors (iliopsoas, rectus femoris).

Anatomic Focus

Hand position: Put your hands behind your head and grasp the bench for support.

Foot position: In the start position, your thighs should be vertical and your lower legs parallel to the bench so that you have a 90-degree bend at your knees and hips. Keep your feet and legs together.

Body position: Keep your upper torso in contact with the bench.

Range of motion: Contract your lower abs to lift your pelvis up off the bench, raising your legs until your toes point to the ceiling.

VARIATION

Hip Flexor Machine

Hip flexor machines allow you to perform a supine leg raise variation of the reverse crunch with resistance in the form of a strap across your lower thighs.

Twisting Sit-Up

FINISH

Rectus abdominis

Serratus anterior

External oblique

START

Execution

1. Sit on the decline bench, hook your feet under the pad, lean back, and position your hands behind your head.
2. As you sit up, twist your torso, directing your right elbow toward your left knee.
3. Lower back down to the start; during the next repetition direct your left elbow toward your right knee.

Muscles Involved

Primary: Rectus abdominis, obliques.

Secondary: Serratus anterior, hip flexors.

Anatomic Focus

Hand position: Position your hands behind your head.

Foot position: Your feet must be secured under a roller pad or comparable support.

Body position: Knees should be bent to reduce stress on the lower back.

Range of motion: Your torso should be vertically upright in the top position, with one elbow almost touching the opposite knee. Lower your torso backward until almost parallel to the floor, about three-quarters of the way down. If you lean back too far, tension is released from the abdominal muscles and more stress is placed on the lower back.

Trajectory: Tilting the bench at a steeper angle makes the exercise harder.

Resistance: Increase resistance by tilting the bench at a steeper incline or holding a small weight plate behind your head.

VARIATION

Broomstick Twist

Sit upright on the edge of a flat bench while holding a broomstick behind your neck. Twist your upper body from side to side. When you twist to the right, feel the right oblique muscles contract, and vice versa.

Oblique Crunch

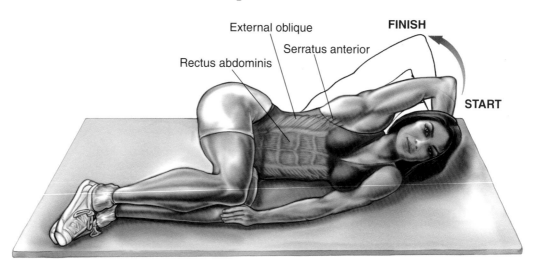

Execution

1. Lie on your left side, knees bent together, right hand behind your head.
2. Slowly lift your upper body by contracting your right-side obliques.
3. Lower your torso back down.

Muscles Involved

Primary: Obliques, rectus abdominis.

Secondary: Serratus anterior.

Anatomic Focus

Hand position: Place your upper-side hand behind your head and rest the other hand over your knee for balance. Do not pull your neck up with your hand.

Foot position: Position your feet so that you have almost a 90-degree bend at your knees and hips. Keep your legs together.

Body position: Lie on your left side to work the right obliques, and then switch to lie on your right side to work the left obliques. Perform this exercise on a cushioned exercise mat placed on the floor.

Range of motion: Your torso crunches 30 to 45 degrees upward from the floor.

VARIATIONS

Incline Oblique Crunch

Use an incline abdominal chair. Secure your feet on the support platform and lean back sideways into the seat, resting on one buttock only. Place your uppermost hand behind your head, and crunch your torso upward.

Additional variation:

Machine oblique crunch: Perform this while sitting obliquely in the seat of a crunch machine, working one side at a time.

Cable Oblique Crunch

START

FINISH

Serratus anterior

Rectus abdominis

External oblique

Execution

1. Grab a D-handle attached to the high pulley of a cable machine.
2. Crunch downward, directing your elbow toward the opposite knee.
3. Slowly return to the start position.

Muscles Involved

Primary: Obliques, serratus anterior.

Secondary: Rectus abdominis.

Anatomic Focus

Hand position: Your hand should grasp the handle above or alongside your head.

Foot position: You may perform this exercise while standing, kneeling, or sitting.

Body position: You can perform this exercise while facing toward or away from the weight stack, depending on personal preference.

Range of motion: Your torso should move from the upright position to almost parallel with the floor.

Resistance: Alter resistance by adjusting the weight stack.

VARIATIONS

Standing Oblique Cable Crunch

Stand sideways to the weight stack, grab the D-handle attached to a high pulley with your nearside hand, and crunch downward, directing your elbow to the hip.

Additional variation:

Rope oblique crunch: Holding the rope attachment with both hands (as described on page 168), crunch with a twist to one side and then the other to work the obliques. The motion is similar to that used during twisting sit-ups.

Dumbbell Side Bend

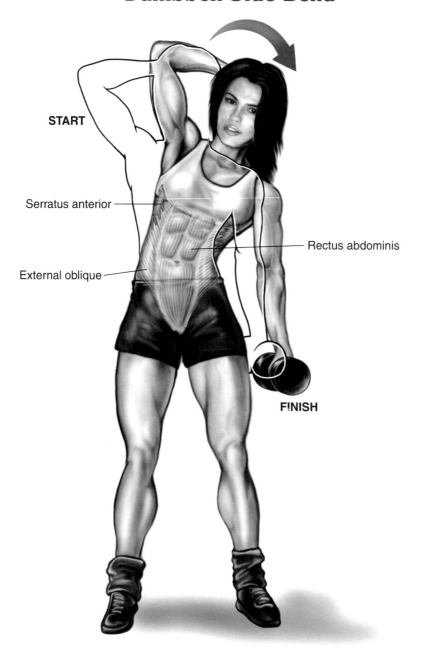

START

Serratus anterior

Rectus abdominis

External oblique

FINISH

Execution

1. Stand upright while holding a dumbbell in your left hand and place your right hand behind your head.
2. Bend your torso to the left side, lowering the dumbbell toward your knee.
3. Straighten your torso upright, contracting the right oblique muscles.

Muscles Involved

Primary: Obliques, serratus anterior.

Secondary: Rectus abdominis, quadratus lumborum

Anatomic Focus

Hand position: Hold a dumbbell at arm's length by your side in one hand, and place the other hand behind your head.

Foot position: Stand with your feet hip-width apart.

Body position: When you bend to the right side, you work the left obliques, and vice versa.

Range of motion: Your torso should bend approximately 45 degrees or until the dumbbell becomes level with your knee.

Trajectory: Your torso should move directly sideways without leaning to the front or back.

Resistance: Avoid using a heavy dumbbell for this exercise. Large overdeveloped oblique muscles will make your waist appear bulky.

VARIATION

Cable Side Bend

Use a D-handle attached to a low pulley and stand side-on to the weight stack.

Dumbbell Pullover

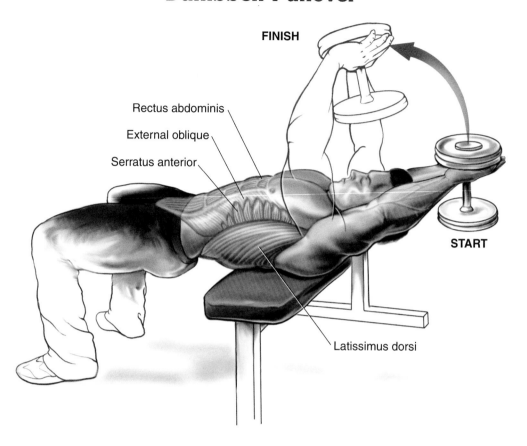

FINISH

Rectus abdominis

External oblique

Serratus anterior

START

Latissimus dorsi

Execution

1. Lie with your upper back resting across a flat bench; hold a dumbbell straight above your chest.
2. Lower the dumbbell down and backward until it reaches bench level, inhaling deeply and stretching your rib cage.
3. Pull the weight back up to the vertical position, exhaling as you do so.

Muscles Involved

Primary: Serratus anterior, intercostals, latissimus dorsi.

Secondary: Pectorals, triceps.

Anatomic Focus

Grip: Hold the dumbbell by placing your palms against the inside of the weight plate at one end, making a diamond shape around the bar with your thumbs and index fingers.

Body position: Your torso should remain still and parallel to the floor, with your upper back resting on the bench and your feet firm on the floor for stability.

Range of motion: The dumbbell moves through an arc of about 90 degrees. Aim for a full stretch in your rib cage as the weight is lowered.

Resistance: Do not use a heavy weight, because the shoulder joint is vulnerable to injury during this exercise. This is not an exercise for the oblique muscles. It is included in this section because the serratus anterior is worked during most oblique exercises.

VARIATION

Barbell Pullover

This is the same exercise using a barbell. Machine pullover is another variation.

EXERCISE INDEX

SHOULDERS

CHEST

BACK

ARMS

LEGS

ABDOMINALS

ABOUT THE AUTHOR

Dr. Nick Evans, MD, is an orthopedic surgeon specializing in sports medicine and is a highly regarded authority on strength training, nutrition, and weight-training injuries. He is an expert in musculoskeletal anatomy and has written for numerous scientific publications.

A bodybuilder and fitness model, Evans is also the author of *Men's Body Sculpting*. He writes a monthly "Ask the Doctor" column for *MuscleMag International* and is a columnist for *Oxygen* women's fitness magazine.

Evans resides in Los Angeles, California.

ABOUT THE ILLUSTRATOR

William P. Hamilton is a medical illustrator with extensive anatomical training and 30 years of experience. He illustrates kinesiology columns in *Muscular Development*, *Fitness Rx for Women*, and *Fitness Rx for Men*, and he has written articles and done illustrations for *Pure Power* magazine. Additionally, Hamilton has more than 40 years of weightlifting and bodybuilding experience, having competed in both disciplines. He holds a master's degree (postbaccalaureate certificate, or PBC) in medical illustration from The Ohio State University, is a board-certified medical illustrator (CMI), and serves as an active member of the Association of Medical Illustrators, Graphic Artists Guild, and Guild of Natural Science Illustrators. Hamilton resides in Marquette, Michigan, with his wife, Jacqueline.

ANATOMY SERIES

Each book in the *Anatomy Series* provides detailed, full-color anatomical illustrations of the muscles in action and step-by-step instructions that detail perfect technique and form for each pose, exercise, movement, stretch, and stroke.

THIRD EDITION
Strength Training Anatomy
OVER 1 MILLION COPIES SOLD!
Frédéric Delavier

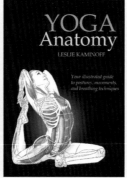

YOGA Anatomy
LESLIE KAMINOFF
Your illustrated guide to postures, movements, and breathing techniques

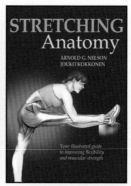

STRETCHING Anatomy
ARNOLD G. NELSON
JOUKO KOKKONEN
Your illustrated guide to improving flexibility and muscular strength

Women's Strength Training Anatomy
Your illustrated guide to shape and tone
• abs
• back
• legs
• buttocks
Frédéric Delavier
Author of *Strength Training Anatomy*

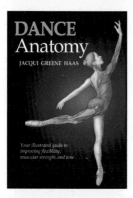

DANCE Anatomy
JACQUI GREENE HAAS
Your illustrated guide to improving flexibility, muscular strength, and tone

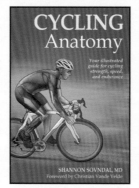

CYCLING Anatomy
Your illustrated guide for cycling strength, speed, and endurance
SHANNON SOVNDAL, MD
Foreword by Christian Vande Velde

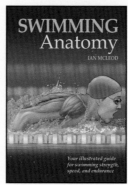

SWIMMING Anatomy
IAN MCLEOD
Your illustrated guide for swimming strength, speed, and endurance

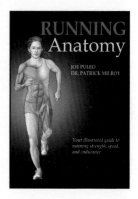

RUNNING Anatomy
JOE PULEO
DR. PATRICK MILROY
Your illustrated guide to running strength, speed, and endurance

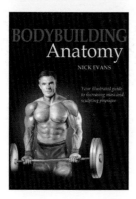

BODYBUILDING Anatomy
NICK EVANS
Your illustrated guide to increasing mass and sculpting physique

POSTERS

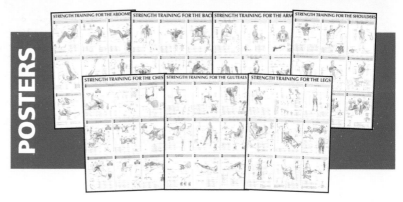

STRENGTH TRAINING FOR THE ABDOME
STRENGTH TRAINING FOR THE BACK
STRENGTH TRAINING FOR THE ARM
STRENGTH TRAINING FOR THE SHOULDERS
STRENGTH TRAINING FOR THE CHES
STRENGTH TRAINING FOR THE GLUTEALS
STRENGTH TRAINING FOR THE LEGS

To place your order, U.S. customers call TOLL FREE **1-800-747-4457**
In Canada call 1-800-465-7301 • In Europe call +44 (0) 113 255 5665 • In Australia call 08 8372 0999
In New Zealand call 0800 222 062 • or visit **www.HumanKinetics.com/Anatomy**

HUMAN KINETICS
The Premier Publisher for Sports & Fitness
P.O. Box 5076, Champaign, IL 61825-5076